Life Skills for Teens

How to Cook Make Friends Be Self Confident

(How to Manage Everyday Life Including Money Management Social Skills)

Jimmy Burris

I0558338

Published By **Elena Holly**

Jimmy Burris

Life Skills for Teens: How to Cook Make Friends Be Self Confident (How to Manage Everyday Life Including Money Management Social Skills)

ISBN 978-1-998927-76-0

No part of this guidebook shall be reproduced in any form without permission in writing from the publisher except in the case of brief quotations embodied in critical articles or reviews.

Legal & Disclaimer

Table Of Contents

Chapter 1: What Are Life Skills?

Life capabilities are the abilities you want to deal with ordinary life. They encompass practical abilities like cooking, budgeting, and managing a while correctly, in addition to interpersonal capabilities like communication, control competencies and teamwork.

Why are life talents so essential for young adults?

Teens need lifestyles abilities to help them transition into adulthood. Without those talents, you may battle to address the needs of normal life. And you can moreover discover it hard to shape healthy relationships and gather your goals or worst; you can no longer be able to get a method and hold a roof over your head, an awful lot an awful lot much less feed and dress yourself. Learning life capabilities is essential for young adults. It does now not depend whether or not or now not or now not you're despite the fact that in university, university, or college, in any other case you've left home – those abilties are important for all and sundry.

I remember one incident as quickly as I become sixteen once I struggled with time management. I had an entire lot of homework to do, but I additionally preferred to spend time with my buddies. I ended up staying up overdue in search of to get the whole thing finished, and then I felt exhausted day after today and could not recognition on college. If I had mentioned approximately time manage techniques decrease lower back then, I need to have saved myself lots of pressure!

I recognize teens are in a hard level of lifestyles as they broaden. I actually have found maximum young adults are looking for to determine out what they want from lifestyles and the manner to navigate the waters of relationships. I too, dealt with this catch 22 situation. Along the way, you could sense frustrated and pressured, especially if to procure right here from a records wherein your parents might not have taught you those gadgets. But I am proper here to tell you; It is our interest as adults or mentors to help guide teenagers (like your self) through this difficult time via teaching crucial lifestyles talents. This e book will teach you seven realistic competencies each teenager want to apprehend to stay extra correctly.

Being empowered and independent for the duration of this diploma is vital. Independent in this example is being mature and expressing your individuality and identification. Learning and getting to know the ones competencies can lessen your frustration, confusion, and anxiety.

Here are the 7 maximum vital ones we are capable of be discussing in this e-book:

1. Communication talents

2. Interpersonal and Intra-private competencies

three. Self-Discovery

4. Creative questioning

five. Time manipulate

6. Decision-making

7. Leadership Abilities

Each financial disaster gives practical pointers and take-movement sports activities to get you training what you observe. By reading this e book, you may advantage the know-how and equipment you need to attain the ones areas shifting earlier into your character existence. These lifestyles talents will assist you acquire fulfillment no longer genuinely to your teenagers however to your grownup lifestyles. So, what are you waiting for? Let's bounce proper in!

Communication Skills and How to Improve Them

Good conversation competencies are critical for forming healthful relationships with others. Whether you're talking to a friend, instructor, or determine, it's critical to realise how to talk efficiently with them. We are all in a time of age in which there is lots of various techniques human beings precise their verbal exchange competencies. For instance, the way we communicate on the cellphone has advanced into texting on cell telephones with extraordinary abbreviations and emojis we although want the critical lesson on communique to enhance our conversation competencies.

Communication is the manner of changing facts amongst or more human beings. This technique which you want as a way to supply and get preserve of messages an splendid manner to speak successfully. To do that, you want to apprehend the perfect methods that you can percentage.

The Three Main Ways to Communicate

There are 3 primary strategies that you can talk:

•Verbal

•Nonverbal

•Written

Verbal communique is whilst you use words to speak. Nonverbal verbal exchange is at the equal time as you use your frame language and facial expressions to talk. Written verbal exchange is whilst you use letters, emails, or textual content messages to speak. Each form of verbal exchange has its very own set of guidelines that you want to understand in case you want to be powerful. So, facts them will help you exercising and examine them.

Firstly, verbalize your thoughts really, and use quick, smooth sentences. Be clean and concise while you communicate and avoid using difficult words or slang terms even as possible. It's additionally important to use accurate grammar and pronunciation whilst you communicate. Sloppy grammar and pronunciation can make it difficult for others to understand you. Yes, I understand every so often at the same time as you get round buddies there may be a second you may stray off because of the truth it's miles a cool factor to talk in slang but make certain to talk properly and slowly as you are pronouncing your phrases at the same time as it is suitable.

When it involves nonverbal communique, be privy to your frame language and facial expressions. Make certain that you're sending the proper message together with your body language. For example, if you're angry or disillusioned, don't attempt to fake that you're happy thru smiling. Your facial expressions will come up with away.

Also, be privy to the signs that you're sending together at the side of your frame language. Crossed arms and legs can advise that you're uncomfortable or closed off from the character you're speaking to. Leaning a long way from someone or turning your body away also can show which you're no longer interested in what they have got to mention. Finally, in terms of written communication, make certain to proofread your work before sending it out. Typos and errors can be corrected proper away at that 2d if you see them inside the route of your proofreading time. Also, the use of the not unusual dispositions of social media acronyms and abbreviations ought to make it tough for others to understand what you're attempting to say.

Not each technology may be aware about those expressions, so keep in mind to use them whilst it is suitable. Taking the time to study over your paintings carefully is a simple key and proscribing using acronyms and abbreviations to while they will be because it should be is a start. Now that we protected the fundamentals of conversation, permit's deep dive into extra techniques to decorate your verbal exchange ability.

My Story About Communicating

But first, I want to proportion a quick tale about myself.

When I grow to be a teenager developing up, I struggled with talking with my dad and mom and teachers approximately problems I faced as I became analyzing new matters in school, I take delivery of as genuine with I turn out to be a sluggish learner, and I wasn't maintaining the brand new stuff I grow to be mastering. If it wasn't interesting to me, I wasn't listening. I decided it hard to find out the phrases to specific what I wanted to say, or even extra difficult for me to mention them out loud to my dad and mom, no matter the reality that I became said to speak lots in immoderate school however handiest as it became things I ought to narrate to among my friends. Can you relate to my tale?

I felt like my parents or teachers might in reality brush me off or no longer pay attention to me if I did manipulate to mention some component. So, most of the time I just stored my thoughts and feelings to myself, which prompted a whole lot of pent-up frustration wherein I surely fell quick in doing what they requested.

Deep down speaking have emerge as an area of disconnect for me as a teen due to the reality in my case I favored to understand things like high-quality topics I felt had been difficult and lifestyles in preferred from a youngster's factor of view. If you're struggling with similar communication problems, don't worry, you're no longer on my own. It's perfectly everyday to have trouble speaking as a teenager. But the high-quality statistics is there may be preference that you could beautify your conversation abilities and cultivate right relationships at some point of existence. And God is aware about you will need this transferring beforehand into adulthood.

Here are the pinnacle 4 most essential tactics to decorate communication. Also, check out the exercising to workout what you learned.

1. Listen extra than you speak

This is probably the most critical tip on the listing. I struggled with this as a teenager. Sometimes even as an grownup, I get decrease lower returned into my awful dependancy of doing this. I do remind myself to bear in thoughts of this however don't get difficult on myself if I don't get it right. So, learning to pay attention more even as in a communique, speaks volumes and, indicates the alternative person that you are trying to concentrate to what they're announcing. Doing this will now not simplest lead them to sense heard and valued, but it will additionally offer you with a better information in their attitude. It may be tough to try this, specifically in case you're used to talking extra than you pay interest, it's sad however proper that's what I have become seemed for. Make sure you try your incredible to attention on the possibility person and what they're pronouncing.

Chapter 2: Intra-Personal And Interpersonal Skills: What Are They, And The Manner Do You Tell Them Aside?

Have you ever puzzled what makes teens accurate at socializing? Is it their individual, or the way they carry themselves? It may be a piece of every, however more often than not, it's their interpersonal capabilities that set them apart. Interpersonal competencies are the skills we use to interact with others. They encompass things like conversation, empathy, teamwork, and emotional intelligence. On the alternative hand, intrapersonal skills are the abilities we use to interact with ourselves. How we address ourselves shows on how we deal with others is high. They moreover encompass such things as self-cognizance, self-law (strength of will) and mindfulness. Young adults with robust intrapersonal capabilities are often introspective and have a deep records in their very very personal thoughts and emotions.

The term "intrapersonal" surely way "internal." People with robust intrapersonal talents are unique at expertise their personal feelings, goals, and needs. They're moreover appropriate at placing private obstacles and coping with their very own emotions. While intrapersonal competencies are essential for young adults (and all and sundry else), they don't continuously come genuinely. In truth, many teens conflict with self-attention, self-love, and emotional law. The precept proper right here for intrapersonal is loving yourself first not in a selfish conceited way but due to the truth you could only love one of a kind human beings to the quantity as you like yourself.

In assessment, the term "interpersonal" comes from the Latin phrase "inter," due to this between, and "person," meaning person or masks. In unique phrases, interpersonal competencies are the trends we use while we've interaction with different humans. While each devices of talents are vital, intrapersonal competencies are greater important in a teenager's social life. As we undergo youth, we're trying to find to discern out who we are and in which we in shape in. But turning our thoughts onto self-care and loving ourselves first permits us to like others and cope with others how we want to be dealt with. After all, we can't have wholesome relationships with others if we don't apprehend the manner to speak or apprehend their emotions.

The key distinction among intrapersonal and interpersonal abilities

So, what's the difference among those two styles of talents? And how can you inform if a person has them?

Let's take a better appearance.

The important difference among intrapersonal and interpersonal abilties is that intrapersonal abilities are focused on our inner worldwide, on the same time as interpersonal abilties are targeted on our out of doors global.

If you need to beautify your intrapersonal skills, there are some subjects you can do. First, get to recognize your self higher with the aid of the use of taking some time to soul-are trying to find. Second, paintings on constructing your arrogance and self guarantee. Finally, set dreams for yourself and try and fulfill them. Good interpersonal abilties are essential in each your private home, your manner and your educational adventure. If you want to beautify your interpersonal capabilities, there are a few subjects you can do. First, paintings on your communique skills. Second, attempt to see topics from the other individual's angle. Finally, be assertive and discover ways to take care of confrontations maturely together with your pals.

Why are intrapersonal and interpersonal capabilities important?

Intrapersonal and interpersonal skills are each crucial due to the truth they can help you take manage of your life and construct strong relationships. After years of no longer data myself, I decided to cognizance on developing my intrapersonal abilties. Once I started out to get a higher enjoy of who I became and what I desired out of life, the entirety else began to fall into location. My relationships started out out to decorate, and I vast absolutely felt happier.

If you're struggling in any place of your existence, whether it's school, your part-time mission, or your relationships, focusing on your intrapersonal or interpersonal skills could make a large difference. Additionally, for me as quickly as I actually have grow to be really targeted on what I favored to do with my life, my intrapersonal capabilities kicked in and helped me set desires to advantage something first-rate like writing this e book to effect and assist guide the subsequent generation. Interpersonal capabilities are particularly wanted in the teenage years as it's far a time of extremely good trade and transition. It's sooner or later of the ones years which you leave formative years at the back of and start to form your personal identification and friendships. You begin to this point, get jobs, or visit university. You moreover ought to cope with such things as peer stress and heartbreak. All of these critiques may be overwhelming, but if you have sturdy interpersonal skills, you'll be better ready to deal with them.

One of the exceptional approaches to increase interpersonal skills is to get involved in extracurricular sports. Doing things like gambling sports activities sports, turning into a member of a club, or volunteering let you discover ways to work properly with others and remedy conflicts. Additionally, those sports activities provide a high-quality opportunity to exercise your communication abilities.

So, how will you inform if a person has those super abilties?

To sum it up another time, intrapersonal talents are approximately statistics oneself, whilst interpersonal competencies are approximately information others. As for telling whether or now not or no longer or not someone has the ones skills, it could be a hint complicated. However, one nicely way to determine that is with the aid of searching at their conduct in unique situations. For instance, do they get along properly with people, or do they seem shy and withdrawn? Another issue to do not forget is how well they deal with stress and difficult conversations.

If someone can live calm below stress and communicate effectively even when topics get tough, then bingo! Probabilities are they've got sturdy interpersonal abilities. If you're interested in developing your personal intrapersonal or interpersonal skills, there are plenty of techniques you can do.

Check out the take movement internet net page for a few thoughts!

TAKE ACTION:

1.Take some time to reflect on your very non-public intra-non-public and interpersonal skills. What are your strengths and weaknesses in those regions?

2.Make a listing of goals you need to accumulate in phrases of your intrapersonal or interpersonal skills. For instance, you can need to artwork on being extra assertive or being a higher listener.

3.Find opportunities to workout your talents. For instance, if you're shy, attempt setting up a conversation with a stranger. Or if you need to be better at dealing with battle, attempt role-playing fantastic situations with a chum.

four. Seek out property to be able to allow you to improve your abilties. There are loads of books, articles, and websites that offer recommendation on developing intrapersonal and interpersonal skills. Do some studies and discover some that you assume may be useful.

five. Be affected man or woman with your self. It takes time to enlarge strong intrapersonal and interpersonal abilities. It felt this way for me. Don't get discouraged if you don't see outcomes right away. Just hold running at it and you'll in the end get there I promise. So don't wait any greater, start working on them these days!

Self-Discovery and Tips to Become More Aware of Yourself

Let me ask you this…

How well do you realize yourself?

What alternate do you need to see to your life?

Who do you want to become?

These are crucial questions to ask oneself to have interaction in self-discovery. To emerge as more privy to ourselves, we want to be sincere with ourselves first and take an honest take a look at our mind, emotions, and attitudes. Many humans go through life without ever taking the time to explore who they're and what makes them whole, separate, and particular. As a stop result, they emerge as dwelling a lifestyles that isn't always genuine to them and regularly enjoy unfulfilled. When you appearance again into records, you may find out that many awesome human beings took the time to find out themselves. They explored their passions, tap into their capacity, and found out their strengths, and weaknesses which in turn used the know-a way to create lives which have been actual, influential, impactful, and excellent.

Even in ancient Greek history, there was a proverb that proclaims, "understand thyself", it is inscribed at the temple of Apollo in Delphi. This is a completely important announcing as it manner that if you want to understand who you are and what you want in existence, you want to understand yourself first. It is best while you understand your self that you may begin making options which can be proper for you and not based mostly on a person else's opinion. You have to discover ways to consider your capabilities and the deep choice for motive inside, then you can locate the whole thing else falls into place.

Another quote that speaks volumes approximately the statistics of self-discovery is through a philosopher named Socrates. He is idea for announcing "To recognise thy self is the start of know-how". This is a powerful fact, to reiterate this if you don't apprehend who you are, then how can you are making smart selections?

You have to be aware of your mind, inner feelings, ideals, and values to make choices which can be right for you. It is handiest at the same time as you come to be greater aware of your self that you may start living a life this is proper to you.

What is the importance of self-discovery for young adults and teens?

Teens and young adults advantage considerably from self-discovery. It lets in them to find out their abilities, items, and abilities. It additionally permits them figure out what they will be captivated with and develop a sturdy experience of identification which in flip uncovers their motive and a experience of leadership in life. You can thrive as a young character on your areas of gifting & competencies and talents and not using a apologies. Tapping into your God-given, limitless capability to make contributions your lifestyles work to the following technology is your management.

Reiterating what I stated earlier than approximately self-discovery is the riding stress that permits you to move deep into pinpointing what you are enthusiastic about and that is wherein you mild up inner. This is wherein the advantages of discovering oneself kick in. You in the mean time are absolutely conscious and empowered with the useful resource of your skills, functionality and strengths you benefit without a doubt with the aid of getting clarity and expertise of your traits, dispositions, emotions, desires and values. In the long time, this blessings you to make clever choices that will help you set goals and acquire your goals.

Self-Discovery is taking a deeper plunge into exploring your truths and uncovering additives of yourself which you were formerly ignorant of. It may be hard but profitable, it is able to take the time, however you are greater than in a function, organized, and authorized to embark in this adventure as you return to recognize greater approximately who you are and what makes you specific. You can also moreover come upon some adults that would say "Oh your too more youthful to do this" however it's miles in no way too late to start taking duty for developing your private existence and desires and all of this starts offevolved offevolved with coming across your self. Before you can expect to broaden and alternate into the individual you preference, it's critical to recognize your reason or calling (the aspect that you choice to do). However, deep down internal for some young adults, it can be tough to discover because of a loss of assist and guidance. But simplest when you have a clear and impartial view of yourself you can go with the flow beforehand to start putting practical goals to convey that individual you desire and the art work you select to do into fact.

So, if you're organized, Let's take some time to find out who you are and what makes you precise. The rewards can be properly surely really worth it!

What are a few recommendations for developing self-attention?

Here are 8 brief guidelines to begin your adventure of growing self-interest:

1.Pay hobby in your thoughts and emotions. Be honest with your self approximately what you want and don't like, what makes you excited and what stresses you out. Also, discover your pursuits- What matters do you experience doing? What sparks your hobby? What are you obsessed on?

2.Take time for self-mirrored photo. Spend time on my own each day thinking about your past, present and destiny. Grab a mag with or without set off questions and jot down any mind that might come. What are your dreams and aspirations? What do you want to gain in lifestyles?

3.Get to understand your tendencies and your person kind. Everyone has their very own precise set of personality tendencies, that have an effect on the manner they suppose, revel in, and behave. Make a list of your characteristics and located them at the vanguard of everything you do. As on your personality type, there are numerous great loose persona tests to be had at the net and books in this issue be counted at your close by library. The one I will advise is the Myers-Briggs check for teenagers. (Google this name) it's far going to be a test to help you to understand your person type. Once you understand what type of person you are, it's far going to be less complex as a way to choose out your strengths and weaknesses constant with the person kind you discover.

Chapter 3: Methods Of Self-Discovery

There are numerous diverse strategies for teenagers to investigate greater approximately themselves thru techniques which might be tapping into their ideas, mind, and emotions. I already factor out this thru the recommendations furnished however this approach have become my desired, and that is journaling.

Journaling lets in you to song your mind and feelings through the years, and to appearance how they alternate and develop. This will assist you apprehend yourself higher. I can attest to this from my very very own experience. It will come up with a place to file your journey. The extremely good component is to have the right concept-scary questions to answer.

A few prompt questions will reason your mind to expect and dig deeper to locate that hidden conviction you had from teens to guide you inside the right direction. It may be a region to find out feelings with out judgment or pressure, which will become a healing tool that enables you release difficult feelings.

Another manner is thru mindfulness meditation. In mindfulness meditation, you attention at the winning 2d to be aware about your mind and emotions as they rise up. Just like I said in tip #6 of growing self-attention, this too is a Spiritual Connection. Anybody can do meditation- younger or antique. What you will be meditating on is your connection for your desires.

These goals are the thoughts of what you want out of lifestyles which incorporates your emotions in the direction of them. If you are wondering and speaking to them into being via faith(perception) Then you're aligning your desires together together with your phrases. This is wherein vision forums and visualization physical sports can come into play. Visualizing to your thoughts the ones vital belongings you need to do and connecting your feelings and desires to take transport of as real with the image you spot goes to come decrease back to skip, it's far already finished, it's going to appear, it is ready to arise.

The excellent way to tie this all in is to think about the belongings you cherish and love in lifestyles. Focus on those desires as if you are already residing them. To sum all of it up, actually recall, if you could see it for your thoughts or imagination then you can have it in your existence. This method, if executed right will assist you to learn how to tune into your highbrow pix and take what is in your mind to fact. The gain of that is selling calmness and clarity of concept. I understand this can sound out of region for teens, however you may be surprised whilst you start searching inward in choice to outward from your external factors.

The Importance of comments from others

To gain a extra well-rounded records of ourselves, it's far essential to are seeking out comments from others. This may be tough, as it may be frightening to pay attention what others consider us. However, it's far vital to consider that remarks– whether or no longer or now not splendid or poor – is a precious tool for growth.

To accumulate remarks correctly, it's miles important to create an surroundings in which the alternative person feels consistent and cushty (No rely who the individual is). This manner being open to being attentive to what your dad and mom or teachers have to say, without judgment or getting defensive. It is likewise essential to be clear approximately what sort of feedback you're looking for. For instance, in case you are struggling with a specific problem, you can ask for unique tips about the way to address it.

By analyzing to gather comments effectively, you may benefit a better know-how of your self and assist others to do the equal. To finish this economic catastrophe on self-discovery, it's miles important to don't forget that that is an ongoing adventure, and the purpose is truly to turn out to be extra aware of who you're so that you can live a existence that is real and applicable. There isn't any "right" or "wrong" manner to do it, and there may be no holiday spot which you want to acquire apart from your real purpose and staying in your lane.

The guidelines and suggestions on this bankruptcy are presupposed to be a start line – a way to get you thinking about the manner of self-discovery. There are many extraordinary belongings available, as a manner to discover which consist of my on line mini path "How to Identify your Why". This mini route is a unfastened gift to you, to start your adventure take a look at out the property internet web page at the back of the e-book for delivered records.

TAKE ACTION:

Let's pull out a piece of paper or a favourite mag and solution those questions.

Remove all distractions and locate someplace quiet. This workout calls for your complete interest you have to take a seat down and suppose!

Let's start out with Five pinpointing questions:

1. What is your internal most desire?

•The deep-seated belongings you want to do the maximum in lifestyles.

2. What are your passions?

•Think approximately things that energized and moderate you up

three. What makes you angry?

•Think approximately topics which you hold in thoughts unjust or unsatisfactory

4. What do you want you may trade about the world?

•Imagine yourself growing a distinction what does that appear like

five. What mind or mind are chronic?

•Have you perception of any innovations or agency thoughts any famous mind that preserve coming back time and again over again?

WHAT TO LOOK FOR...

Highlight normal similarities for your responses.

•comparable solutions are to verify what you were designed to do in (Purpose)

•Different answers to each question suggest the need for extra readability on your responses.

•Don't fear too much in case you are having problem identifying any of the questions.

•take a smash and go returned at the same time as you feel is extraordinary and suitable.

Discovering purpose does take the time. Don't give up-Keep pressing earlier with perseverance. Some of the questions require you to contemplate a piece bit longer for readability. Don't overlook to evaluate and put together your findings with Tip #three of the 8 brief recommendations for developing self-consciousness.

Creative wondering: The Importance and Innovative guidelines

Wfowl I have become growing up, I changed into by no means suggested that I can be creative or that my mind mattered. It wasn't until I actually have become older and well into adulthood that I positioned out the power of revolutionary wondering. Going through my self-discovery journey allowed me to Identify my writing capabilities and consequently ignited my calling of writing. Once I changed into completely aware of my writing present, I knew in my coronary heart that I painted with words (this is how I are trying to find advice from it) and that introduced happiness to my soul, so my modern juices started out out to go with the flow.

I strongly consider being aware of your abilties gives you the empowerment you need to be assured to percentage your creativity with the world, you recognise that you have a few detail precious to offer. It doesn't depend number huge variety what age you're, it's in no manner too overdue to start questioning creatively and innovatively. Just because you didn't broaden up being cautioned that your mind bear in mind, doesn't recommend they don't. You can despite the fact that hone in to your present day capabilities and allow your self to anticipate out of doors of the container.

It's vital to discover your creativity as it lets in you to be more revolutionary. Innovation is high in these days's society due to the fact we're constantly transferring ahead and evolving. We want to pay hobby an increasing number of young adults being progressive and making and growing outstanding innovations. Now, as a youngster in this day of age, you will be even more contemporary and innovative than ever before. Why? Because you're no longer slowed down with the resource of the policies and expectancies of the character worldwide. You can assume outside the sector and come up with new mind that no character has ever belief of earlier than and gift them on line on a number of the social media structures available. This is a important time for your lifestyles even as you are transitioning from a infant to an grownup.

You are beginning to come to be more unbiased and make your very very own picks. It's important to start questioning creatively and innovatively now so you may be a achievement inside the destiny. There are many things you may do as a youngster to begin wondering extra creatively and innovatively. Use your creativity to give you new thoughts, start a fashion, or definitely share your abilities with the area but you choice. Who is aware of, you could certainly inspire a person else to be greater progressive and revolutionary as properly.

Chapter 4: What Is Creative Thinking?

So, how can you be more creative?

First, you need to understand what innovative wondering is. Creative wondering is the capability to look matters in a cutting-edge manner, provide you with new mind, and locate new answers to issues. This is why I keep saying It's approximately wondering outdoor the sphere and being open to new possibilities. As a teenager, you are not told to enter the area and remedy problems creatively and innovatively.

But that is why I am right proper here to tell you; you could though be extra youthful and make a distinction in this manner. One of the great techniques to come to be extra progressive is to surround your self with specific revolutionary people. Spend time with buddies who are into artwork, track, or writing. Go to museums and artwork galleries. Listen to new types of music. Read books that encourage you. By exposing yourself to new and numerous matters, you'll begin to see the arena in an entire new manner.

Another outstanding way to decorate your creativity is to tackle new demanding situations. I understand scary right? Something new and difficult can also definitely be the stepping stool had to get you from your consolation region. If you're constantly doing the same matters, you'll in no manner stretch your mind and come up with new thoughts. So, attempt a few component new. Take a completely unique direction to school. Join a club or group which you're no longer sure you'll be right at. Sign up for an art or dance elegance. By pushing your self outside of your consolation location, you'll open your self as much as new opportunities.

Don't be afraid to test. The global is looking forward to your mind. Trust me the region desires them. If you're looking to provide you with a current idea, don't be afraid to attempt some thing that could seem a piece crazy. Sometimes the nice thoughts come from the most unlikely locations. So, pass in advance and write that tale, paint that photo, or assemble that model. You in no manner understand wherein your creativity will take you.

Don't forget about approximately approximately modern wondering is a talent that you could examine and exercise. By using your creativeness and taking on new challenges, you may start to see the region in an entire new way.

The Importance of Creativity

The significance of creativity cannot be overemphasized. It is creativity that helps us to provide you sparkling mind and discover new solutions to problems, it's miles the using stress within the lower back of innovation and development. Creativity is vital for each private and professional increase as you're taking off into adulthood. For human beings, creativity lets in us to find out our passions and specific ourselves in unique strategies. It allows us to investigate, grow, and evolve as human beings. For entrepreneurial agencies, creativity is important for innovation and boom.

It permits companies to stay aggressive and offer you with new products and services that meet the dreams in their customers. Remember creativity is a skills that can be placed and practiced. In case you don't use your modern thinking talents, you'll lose them. So, exit and use your imagination and in no way be afraid to strive some element new. Start seeing the arena for what it is a place to make a contribution to and make a difference. So, pass earlier and be innovative!

How Can Creativity Be Nurtured in Teens?

There are some key subjects that mother and father and educators can do to help nurture creativity in teenagers. One is to provide possibilities for revolutionary expression. This ought to encompass giving them get entry to to art work materials, musical gadgets, or laptop software program program programs that allow for innovative expression. It can also advocate providing possibilities for them to have interaction in modern sports, on the aspect of dance, drama, or writing. Another manner to nurture creativity in teenagers is to foster a progressive surroundings.

This method growing an atmosphere wherein it's miles ok to take dangers and make errors. It approach encouraging them to discover new thoughts and letting them mission the recognition quo. It furthermore approach presenting powerful reinforcement when they display cutting-edge questioning.

Finally, it's far essential to help teenagers learn how to brainstorm or mind map, to provide you with new thoughts. This includes coaching them the manner to assume appreciably and logically, further to the way to offer you modern answers to issues.

The Benefits of being a Creative Thinker

Here is a list:

•Boosts trouble-solving capabilities

•Encourages out-of-the-discipline wondering

•Helps with crucial thinking

•Increases self-self assure and empowers you

•Allows for self-expression

•Develops a experience of creativity and creativeness

How to enhance your Creativity

Here is a recap

•Get stimulated with the beneficial aid of others

Find modern humans to conform with on social media or be a part of of their blogs or newsletters. Be inspired with the useful resource of their work and discover new thoughts to explore.

•Take on new challenges

See what you could give you, challenge yourself to provide you an invention, write a story, or paint a photograph. Push your self outside your comfort vicinity and observe what you may create.

•Practice, exercise, workout

The greater you operate your imagination and flex your innovative muscle agencies, the higher you will become at wondering creatively. So, don't be afraid to check and try new matters.

•Nurture your creativity

Expose your self to new opportunities and research. Take on new demanding situations. Be open to new mind. By doing the ones items, you'll begin to see the world in a current moderate and be greater innovative as a give up stop result.

TAKE ACTION:

Use your creativeness to decorate your creativity.

Here are five strategies to start:

1. Start by way of the usage of manner of having a pipe dream. Think about property you would like to do whether or not or now not it's visiting to a modern vicinity or analyzing a ultra-modern capacity. Daydreaming will will will let you by using way of permitting your thoughts to freely wander and contemplate new mind and inspirations. You'll be surprised at what you provide you with.

2. Use your imagination to visualise yourself achieving your goals. This way picturing your self in distinct conditions to your thoughts and considering how you may

react or experience within the ones situations. Just as I changed into explaining previously in "The Mindful Mediation" section of Methods of Self-discovery. Visualizing yourself achieving your desires permit you to live inspired and at the proper track.

three. Now which you are seeing highbrow snap shots create a imaginative and prescient board out of your visualization to demonstrate what your future may additionally moreover seem like. By doing this, you will be much more likely to do so and make exquisite modifications to your lifestyles.

four. Come up with thoughts for brand spanking new products or services. Think about things which you want for your life but don't currently exist. Challenge your self to layout this prototype. (invention)

•What are a few answers to problems which you face on a every day foundation concerning services and products?

5. And finally proper proper here's a a laugh way to beautify creativity.

•Write a noun that describes your innovative challenge or concept.

•Add two adjectives that describe the noun you virtually wrote.

•Next listing 3 verbs that describe the impact you envision on your assignment or idea making.

Chapter 5: Best Techniques To Manage Your Time More Effectively

I understand how hard it could be to in shape everything in in the end. There are simplest such quite a few hours inside the day, and once in a while it looks like there can be in no manner enough time to get the entirety finished. But there are some subjects that you can do to make the maximum of it slow and to be greater effective collectively along with your time control. I can don't forget one time once I became looking for to examine for a check however also had a whole lot of homework to do. I modified into feeling so beaten and didn't apprehend how I changed into going to get all of it done. But then I calmed my anxiety via talking to myself to reassure myself that I clearly have everything below control.

Then I had been given contemporary. I eventually observed a time table that worked for me and I have become capable of get everything carried out. It wasn't easy, but it became properly really worth it in the long run. There will constantly be times when you have to squeeze topics in, however with a chunk creativity, you could make it artwork. Starting to exercise coping with it slow efficiently will assist you presently and inside the destiny. The commonplace day has only such a number of hours in it, and there are extraordinary such pretty some topics that you can realistically in shape into that issue.

5 Ways to Manage your Time More Effectively

1. Develop a routine

The first approach to manipulate some time greater efficiently is to growth a regular. This way putting apart particular times each day for particular sports, like faculty, homework, sports, and downtime. It's also essential to set dreams and prioritize sports. Figure out which matters are maximum critical to you and then agenda them first. This will assist you live prepared and at the right music.

Time Management plan or recurring for a pupil instance:

7:00 am- Wake up and get geared up for the day

eight:00 am- Leave for college

9:00 am- School starts offevolved offevolved

12:00 pm- Lunch wreck

1:00 pm- School resumes

3:00 pm- End of the college day

4:00 pm- Homework time

five:00 pm- Dinner

6:00 pm- Free time

eight:00 pm- Bedtime

This is nice a famous idea of methods a pupil's day might be scheduled. Of course, there can be days when this time desk received't paintings, and matters will come up. But having a today's plan to conform with will assist you stay on the right track and make the most of it sluggish. Remember, every day is one-of-a-type, and you can need to alter your time table as favored. But if you could learn how to manage some time correctly, it will make a large difference on your lifestyles.

2. Set apart time for every venture

Another manner to govern some time more efficaciously is to set aside time for every challenge and ensure to paste to that point desk as closely as viable. This changed into some thing I achieved to my everyday, and it worked for me, significantly. I should set a selected quantity of time for each venture after which art work on that task till the time emerge as up. Once the time became up, I could float directly to the following assignment understanding complete well I had sufficient time to accomplish that, so I didn't enjoy overwhelmed however happy that I as a minimum finished the mission. This helped me live centered and made my time used because it should be.

So, the key taking proper right here is placing a particular quantity of time for each hobby, after which making sure you end that interest in that set amount of time. Yes, it is able to be hard, at times because of distractions however that's the edge you have had been given of being a younger man or woman, you have greater manage over a while. Depending upon your situation. You can use this to your advantage via setting a time table and sticking to it as carefully as viable.

3. Take breaks

Thirdly, a manner to control a while extra efficaciously is to take breaks. This doesn't imply taking a ruin each five minutes, however instead taking a harm after you've got completed a challenge or after a certain amount of time. This will help you stay focused and avoid burnout.

4. Set desires

Fourthly, set SMART dreams. One way to manipulate it sluggish more correctly is to set dreams. This approach placing specific, measurable, doable, relevant, and time-sure desires. By setting desires, you are capable of degree your improvement and stay on path. This is awesome than putting a agenda because it's extra about what you need to gather in a day, week, or month. For example, your reason might be to finish all of your homework earlier than dinner or to get a terrific grade on a take a look at. Having precise desires will help you live on the right track and endorsed. This method figuring out what you need to perform and then operating towards that goal.

Here are 4 techniques to stay recommended at the same time as pursuing your dreams:

•Plan

When you have a plan, it's less complicated to stay introduced on. This manner knowing what you need to reach your cause after which breaking that down into smaller steps. For instance, in case you want to run a marathon, your plan might be to run three instances in line with week for 6 months. This will assist preserve you on direction and prompted due to the truth you could see your improvement.

•Set last dates

Another manner to live inspired is thru setting ultimate dates. This way giving yourself a specific date by way of way of using which you want to gain your cause. For example, "I want to lose ten kilos with the beneficial resource of the surrender of the month" or "I need to finish my mission with the useful resource of Friday". Having a reduce-off date will help preserve you focused and on the proper song.

•Create a imaginative and prescient board (my favourite)

Visualizing your aim is each other excellent way to live encouraged. As I already noted in previous chapters. All your visualization can set your thoughts as a good deal as recognition to your project handy. Creating a board or list of pictures that represent what you want to collect will considerably effect your thinking about a change. Seeing your goals within the the front of you while instances get difficult will help hold you inspired and stimulated

•Staying first rate and persevering

Finally, staying powerful and persevering are important strategies to live inspired even as pursuing your goals. This method being affected person and by no means giving up. When you stumble upon setbacks, it's essential to research from them and then maintain transferring ahead. Seriously keep moving ahead. Staying high-quality is top as it will preserve you inspired sooner or later of hard instances. And in reality an FYI persevering approach continuing to work hard regardless of the truth that subjects get hard. These attitudes will help you benefit your desires.

5. Prioritize your sports activities

Fifthly, prioritize your sports. This way figuring out what's most essential after which doing that first. For instance, when you have a test developing, you could want to test for that first. Or, when you have a undertaking due, you may want to paintings on that first. Prioritizing your sports will help you operate it slow extra effectively because of the reality you may be walking on the maximum crucial things first. If you exercising the ones tips, you may be able to manage some time greater efficiently. Just don't forget to be affected person and in no way give up. You can do it! So, what are you searching in advance to? Get started the sooner you begin training, the better off you'll be. Trust me, I found the tough way:)

Making normal alternatives: with desire-making pointers

 Making ordinary alternatives may be difficult. Sometimes it seems like there are truely too many options to make, and we don't understand in which to begin. Other instances, we've got an remarkable idea of what we need, but we're now not sure if it's the right preference. How can we make certain that our alternatives are the first-class ones possible?

There's no individual option to that question – absolutely everyone has their method for making assured decisions. But thru studying about special preference-making recommendations, you could test and spot what works for you. In this financial disaster, we'll discover some not unusual strategies I located even as I have turn out to be discovering this topic of the most commonplace technique used by adults in splendid fields of exertions that labored for them in time control. We'll additionally check procedures to deal with tough conditions and conflicting advice. So whether or not you're searching for to select a college or decide what to position on tomorrow, those pointers will assist you sense greater confident for your choices.

The Basics: What is a selection, and Why is it important?

A selection is a preference that you make between or extra options. Every day, we're faced with loads of picks, huge and small. Some – like what to consume for breakfast – are so routine that we don't even consider them. Others – like whether or not or now not to interrupt up together together along with your giant unique – can be life-converting.

Making alternatives is crucial as it's how we shape our lives. The choices we make determine in which we live, what we do for paintings, and who our buddies and circle of relatives are. They moreover have an effect on our fitness, happiness, and fashionable properly-being. That's why it's so crucial to discover ways to make suitable selections. Many humans have problem understanding the electricity of little matters including up. If we make a gaggle of small, lousy alternatives, it could cause huge problem down the road. I don't want to sound judgmental or disrespectful, however for example, permit's say you've been that means to end smoking for a while now. But each time you attempt to give up, you turn out to be relapsing interior in line with week or .

After some time, you'll likely begin to sense adore it's not nicely properly well worth attempting anymore. "I'm simply going to smoke," you may anticipate. "It's not find it irresistible's that huge of a deal." But right proper right here's the element: those little picks add up. If you hold smoking, notwithstanding the truth that you apprehend it's terrible for you, it will harm your fitness. Over time, the ones fitness problems may additionally moreover want to end up severe – or maybe life-threatening. So that one selection won't appear to be a huge deal, but it may have a extremely good effect for your life ultimately.

On the alternative hand, making appropriate choices can bring about a happier, greater healthful, and more a fulfillment life. If you devour healthily, exercise often, and stay a long way from tablets and alcohol, you're more likely to be healthy and satisfied. If you figure tough in university and get right grades, you'll have a higher threat of entering into the college of your preference. And in case you deal with others with appreciate and kindness, you're more likely to have fun relationships.

We all want to do the first-class we can to make best everyday options for 3 foremost motives:

1.   Your Life is predicated upon on it. It improves the exceptional of the lifestyles you stay and barriers strain

2.   Everyday selections shape all your behavior, nicely or lousy which in turn effect your life.

three.   When faced with a tough or emergency choice, it's important to have sturdy preference-making talents.

That manner having a tool in region for comparing your alternatives and developing a preference that you are feeling confident in. By training your desire-making capabilities often, you'll be better organized for tough conditions.

There isn't any character length suits all to you make a decision

One of the maximum crucial topics to don't forget approximately choice-making is that there may be no character proper way to do it. Some humans want to weigh all their options in advance than creating a choice, on the equal time as others prefer to go with their gut intuition. There is not any incorrect way to determine, so long as you're cushty with the very last consequences.

The maximum critical detail is to find a way that works for you. Maybe you like to sleep on huge alternatives earlier than making them, or perhaps you want to talk through your options with a pal. Experiment with awesome techniques and observe what feels superb for you.

Decision-making method

There are dozens of severa choice-making techniques handy, but here are the various maximum famous ones:

Pros and cons: When you're trying to decide among options, it can be useful to make a list of the professionals and cons of each preference. This will will let you appearance the selection greater truly and make a more knowledgeable preference.

Cost-benefit assessment: This method is just like the pros and cons list, however it entails quantifying the expenses and advantages of every alternative. For instance, if you're on the lookout for to determine whether or not or now not to shop for a cutting-edge vehicle or preserve an older hand-me-down automobile, you'll likely listing the fee of a brand new car, the month-to-month bills, the insurance costs, and so forth. You would then take a look at those fees to the benefits of having a modern automobile, similar to the advanced fuel mileage or the guarantee.

Risk assessment: When you're you decide, it's important to recollect the dangers concerned. What are the opportunities that things will pass wrong? How excessive may want to the consequences be? By thinking about the risks, you can make a more informed choice about whether or not to hold.

For example: Make a list of the experts and cons of every choice, and ask your self questions like "Which option is first rate for me?" and "What are the dangers and rewards involved?"

Let's do an example:

1. Deciding whether or not or not to move on a date with a person you met on line:

Pros of taking region the date:

-You can also get to understand a person new and interesting.

-It can also additionally want to result in a current friendship or a excessive dating.

-It's an possibility to have a laugh and find out the metropolis with someone new.

Cons of occurring the date:

-The unique person may be a creep or uninteresting.

-You may also additionally wander away or caught in a terrible a part of metropolis.

-You may additionally want to emerge as spending lots of coins on some trouble you don't experience.

Cost-benefit assessment:

Based on the professionals and cons, it looks as if occurring the date won't be an possibility. But that is an example of the manner to investigate and make your preference. Remember that there is a few chance worried, so you have to weigh the risks and rewards cautiously earlier than making a decision.

Risk evaluation:

The dangers of taking vicinity this date seem notably narrow – there's a small danger that you'll meet someone unstable, however rather, you will probable have a very good time if they may be great and loving. But, you make a decision to move about your choice, manner out the pro and cons first.

2. Deciding whether or not or no longer to transport away domestic to go to a college or college in a special town:

Pros of leaving home:

-You'll get to experience dwelling for your very own.

-You'll meet new humans and make new pals.

-You'll have a look at new things and increase as someone.

Cons of leaving domestic:

-You'll be a long way out of your family and friends.

-FOMO (Fear of lacking out) can also kick in

-It may be luxurious to stay to your own.

Cost-benefit evaluation:

Based on the experts and cons, it looks like the blessings of leaving domestic outweigh the costs. You'll be mastering new subjects and growing as a person, on the identical time as moreover making new buddies and experiencing new topics. However, it's critical to take into account that there are some expenses worried, so you need to weigh the dangers and rewards cautiously in advance than you decide.

Risk evaluation:

The dangers of leaving domestic appear pretty minor – you may probable pass over your circle of relatives and pals a chunk, but that's about it. On the whole, it looks like it's properly without a doubt worth it to move in advance and leave domestic to visit college or university.

These are only a few examples of a manner to efficaciously and successfully make a selection. The technique that works excellent for you'll rely upon the situation and the type of choice you need to make.

How to address tough picks

Some alternatives are tougher to make than others. If you're suffering to choose amongst similarly top alternatives, it may be beneficial to turn a coin or ask a friend for his or her opinion. No, I am in fact kidding! Sometimes, the high-quality detail you may do is take it slow and believe that the proper choice turns into clean in time.

If you're coping with a difficult scenario, like a sick family member or a monetary setback, it can be beneficial to speak to someone like a mentor or a counselor. They can provide guide and steerage as you navigate these hard times.

How to cope with conflicting recommendation

When you're trying to make a desire, you will possibly get conflicting advice from high-quality people. Your parents would possibly will let you recognize one detail, even as your pals can also will allow you to apprehend some issue else. The maximum critical element is to recall your instincts. You understand your self better than absolutely every person else, so that you're the amazing pick of what's proper for you. In the stop, the brilliant character who should make the choice is you. Trust yourself, and apprehend that anything choice you are making, you'll be capable of cope with it. If you're although uncertain, it wouldn't damage to get a second opinion from a person you accept as true with.

Chapter 6: When You Make A Decision You Need A Exchange

Deciding to alternate isn't typically clean, however it's actually really worth it. When you're equipped to make that exchange, proper here are some topics to hold in thoughts:

1. Make a plan:

The first step is to make a plan. What do you need to achieve? How will you circulate about reaching it? Write down your dreams, and offer you with a way for engaging in them.

2. Stay precipitated:

It may be hard to paste on your plan at the same time as topics get tough, but it's crucial to stay stimulated. Find techniques to stay inspired and targeted for your goal. Ideas may additionally encompass setting apart time every day to work for your goal, writing down your development, or surrounding yourself with those who help your goals. Reflect on chapters 3 and five.

3. Persevere:

Change doesn't get up in a unmarried day – it takes time and staying power. Persevere through the tough instances, and don't surrender or abandon your dreams. Remember why you favored to change in the first vicinity, and maintain transferring in advance.

When figuring out whether or no longer or not or no longer to plot to trade, remember to weigh the specialists and cons of the situation. To make an knowledgeable preference, it's miles crucial to collect all of the relevant information.

Pull out a magazine or a piece of paper and answer the subsequent questions:

What are the ability advantages of creating this variation?

What are the capability drawbacks or risks?

How may additionally this variation effect my existence?

What are the viable outcomes of not making this modification?

What belongings am I willing to determine to this change?

Who can help me with this change?

What are my desires for making this change?

What are the capability barriers to growing this transformation?

How should likely I overcome those limitations?

After answering the ones questions, it will be less complex to determine whether or not or no longer or now not or no longer to plan for the trade. If the specialists of making the exchange outweigh the cons, then it's miles probably that making plans for this transformation is the extremely good course of movement. However, if the capability drawbacks or dangers appear too incredible, then it might be super to reconsider. No remember what desire is made, it is critical to remember that exchange may be tough and scary. But with right planning and manual, everybody may want to make a a hit trade in their lifestyles.

There you've got got got it!

Making selections is a everyday a part of life. Sometimes, the options are smooth to make, whilst other instances they're greater difficult. However, through way of using some of the techniques we've discussed, you'll be able to make selections with a piece of good fortune – no matter what the scenario is. Trust your instincts, weigh the specialists and cons, and don't be afraid to invite for help while you need it. With the ones preference-making guidelines, you'll be prepared to cope with a few aspect that comes your manner.

TAKE ACTION:

In a magazine, write down one or choices that you have postponed. Think approximately why you have got got been procrastinating with those particular problems. Write a brief assertion approximately whether or now not you do not forget you studied your hesitation to decide, or act is useful or no longer.

Discovering Your True Leadership Abilities

Tright proper here grow to be a brilliant clever man from a tiny little island of the Bahamas that is 21 miles in period and 7 miles in width that observed his control and hooked up it to many. This guy had a vision and a motive to Transform enthusiasts into leaders and leaders into entrepreneurs of trade. He knew a manner to hold people together to gain some difficulty extra than a commonplace aim. He have become capable of do this via way of speaking his passion, his imaginative and prescient, and his requirements which set up accept as true with and gather relationships. His name emerge as Dr. Myles Munroe. He had pretty fantastic integrity and constantly placed the desires of others earlier than himself. He is understood to be a wonderful leader within the vicinity of locating motive and Leadership schooling and thru doing these items, he turn out to be able to inspire others and make a awesome impact at the area through his many books and teachings on his Youtube channel. Dr. Munroe's art work of coaching a mess of leaders to become themselves has considerably inspired me to do the equal. I can really say He changed into my mentor, and his books modified my lifestyles. Sadly, he and his accomplice and severa others died in a aircraft crash, and that they transition to more heights into a miles-off Kingdom of Glory (heaven). This financial ruin is dedicated to him and his artwork on Leadership. I think that every teen and more youthful adult should understand what real leadership looks like. This is a number of what I absolutely have learned, from him and I need to percent it with you in this economic break.

Leadership is a notable that is quite sought-after in lots of different fields. Whether you need to be the captain of your excessive university soccer group or in a while in existence be a CEO of a exquisite company or a extraordinary network chief on your community location, management capabilities are crucial.

But what does it suggest to be a frontrunner?

How are you capable of find out your control capabilities?

This economic catastrophe offers the opportunity to discover and expand your management abilities. It is all approximately reading what management is, the traits of a success leaders, Overcoming Challenges, and Committing on your thoughts & values and extra.

What is Leadership?

Leadership is the capability to persuade others via idea, generated through a ardour, stimulated by way of a imaginative and prescient, birthed from a conviction, produced by manner of a purpose. -Dr. Myles Munroe

There are many unique definitions of control, but at its center, control is the capability to persuade others with genuine intentions. A leader is likewise a person who is privy to their purpose, is confident in themselves and their capability to benefit their goals and dares to upward push up for what they don't forget in regardless of competition. A chief can be someone who motivates and inspires different people to need to grow to be leaders themselves. They are often visionaries who see the functionality in human beings and occasions, and they may inspire others to artwork together to gain that capacity.

Do you phrase yourself as a leader?

And in the end, a pacesetter is someone who makes use of his or her offers, abilties, and abilties to serve others selflessly to make a terrific effect on society.

In the give up, management is all approximately integrating and coordinating humans, property, and facts to gain that final aim. In other terms, it's about growing a distinction to assist humanity. In his e-book, Becoming a Leader, Dr. Munroe discusses the way of becoming a leader. This method starts offevolved offevolved with growing a private experience of purpose.

Dr. Munroe shows that there are 6 steps to turning into a frontrunner. First, you need to find out your reason in life. This effects in a robust conviction, at the manner that will help you give you a clean vision for the future. Once you've got that imaginative and prescient in mind, it'll ignite your ardour for what you're striving for. And finally, this passion will create a power that evokes others to sign on for you to your adventure of influencing them inside the worldwide of your place of the location for the more specific.

FYI when you have not discovered, that is the definition above however inverted. The truth that that is pronouncing to steer others via using inspiring them collectively along with your vision and goals or thoughts and plans of exchange to make a distinction to help humanity is herbal genius. Young human beings don't have a hassle with inspiring unique friends. They glaringly every day inspire others with out being knowledgeable they need to.

Can you agree?

Dr. Munroe says that we are all leaders irrespective of our age. This manner we will use our capabilities and devices to serve the human beings round us.

Have you found or pinpointed your skills?

Mini Exercise: Pinpointing your Talents and competencies

To discover your control abilities, it's crucial to first perceive your strengths and abilties. What are you first rate at? What do you revel in doing? Think about the matters that make you enjoy excited and stimulated. What receives you fired up? When do you feel maximum alive?

Talents: Your know-how is things you can do resultseasily, and it in no manner adjustments or is going away.

Skills: Something you determined out through the years which brought about you becoming capable from the evaluations or education.

Make a listing of your records/different talents do no longer factor out:

ex. Herbal communicator, Artistic talents or organizing, problem-fixing

Brainstorming Questions:

Once you've got got got a feel of what your strengths and skills are ask yourself: "How can I use them to serve others?"

What are a few procedures you can use your gadgets and competencies to make a tremendous effect on the arena spherical you?

How are you able to begin to increase your management capabilities and start to steer others without a doubt?

Values: a real leader want to personify values

Values are the mind that we select to live with the useful resource of. They assist us make picks and set limitations. Our values decide our movements, attitudes, ethics, and private ideals. Values sharpen you as a actual leader . Values are the inspiration of who you are as a frontrunner. They are the thoughts that you hold high-priced and, more importantly, they may be the subjects which you aren't willing to compromise on. When you understand your values, it becomes an awful lot much much less difficult to make alternatives primarily based on what is crucial to you. You in reality have a basis to stand on even as topics get difficult, and you want to live targeted for your dreams.

Values also assist you to stay authentic to yourself and your beliefs. They provide you with a fixed of hints to stay with the useful resource of and assist keep you accountable. It's critical to keep in mind that our values might also alternate through the years as we develop and take a look at greater approximately ourselves. The secret is to commonly be open to new information and be inclined to make changes if essential.

So, how do you move approximately figuring out your values? One manner is to think about the matters which may be maximum crucial to you in life. What do you care about maximum? What topics maximum to you?

Another manner is to invite yourself what makes you angry or dissatisfied. What do you not tolerate? What do you rise up for irrespective of what? These will be signs and symptoms of your values. Once you've got were given a listing of values, it's essential to reflect on them regularly and make certain they although align with who you're these days.

Brainstorming Questions:

Think approximately what you charge the maximum. Make a list of them.

Chapter 7: Do You Exercise Them To Your Existence?

Examples: company to others, difficult artwork, obligation, duty, faithfulness, and fairness.

Being referred to as to steer is a tall order however it's miles all approximately dwelling a realistic lifestyles. Every man or woman is meant to meet their particular reason (calling) in existence thru manner of responding to the obligation of your manage. You have to be asking your self this query why should I come to be a pacesetter? I am too more youthful too! What if I advised you, it's miles the calling of every person no matter age, gender, instances, or vocation? It's a cause hassle!

In economic destroy three we pointed out how self-discovery and finding reason in existence are so important. And that is what control is all approximately; attractive the cause for that you had been created. I need which you have already answered those

Five pinpointing questions underneath the take motion phase once more in monetary smash 3 due to the truth that became the place to start of your control. If now not pass yet again and answer the questions and started out the device or check the resources net web web page in the back of the e-book to get unfastened get right of get entry to to to to "How to Identify Your Why" the mini-direction that allows you to assist maintain the self-discovery adventure.

Everyone ought to study and broaden their control abilties over the years.

Yes, I stated it! "Everyone" no man or woman is exempt. If you actually believe and understand you've got were given have been given what it takes to be a leader, then you definately definately are proper and so as with the aid of the Creator of the universe.

Many first-rate developments make up a a success chief, permit me reiterate the maximum important ones consist of having a clear imaginative and prescient, being obsessed on what you choose to do, being able to encourage and empower others, and sharing your idea to better your technology are key steps as I said above.

Now that you recognize that everybody has the capacity to be a pacesetter you could now start strolling on growing the ones functions similarly. You also can look for mentors or position models who have developments that you want to emulate.

What Essential Qualities Make Up a Good Leader?

In the e-book, The Spirit of Leadership Dr. Munroe offers a list of a few Essential capabilities that every one suitable leaders want to domesticate through working towards and combining them into their every day life. He says that every one authentic leaders have the following attitudes and inclinations.

•Vision: Good leaders comprehend in which they need to head, thru way of a highbrow image of purpose of their young minds and they might articulate that vision to others in a manner that conjures up them to conform with. In exquisite terms, through method of making a easy photograph for your mind from the intellectual picture of what you want your future to seem like and taking steps to make that manifest.

•Positive mind-set: irrespective of what the scenario looks like they will be targeted on the reason.

•Courage: a frontrunner needs so you can arise for what they agree with in, and now not be worried but inclined to take risks.

•Decision making: a fantastic chief can make tough choices despite the fact that it's no longer popular.

•Creativity: an capability to look an idea to a manner to restore a problem in a brand new and modern manner.

•Flexibility: a leader desires for you to adapt to trade fast.

•Righteous anger: a frontrunner is privy to a manner to get mad for the right motives and stand towards injustice and abuse.

•Humility: being in music with oneself and accepting who they're and willing to investigate from others. Not thinking they may be better than surely actually every person else, not arrogant.

•Integrity: being honest, sincere, and consistent in the whole thing they do with their terms and movements.

•Personal warm temperature: a way and mindset that draws humans and draws the extraordinary out of others.

•Friendship: the functionality to together with one of a kind people with out combating or arguing

•A acceptable self-photograph: a enjoy of nicely-being in oneself, others, and lifestyles

•Sense of humor: the potential to snicker at oneself and lifestyles and now not take lifestyles too appreciably.

•Resilience: the capability to get better after problems stand up is a function of resilient people.

•Passion: a starvation for growth and private improvement

•Self-vicinity: having the capacity and inclined to pay the fee and manage achievement

•Initiative: the capability to find out what desires to be completed and act.

Overcoming Challenges

Leadership isn't continuously easy, and leaders will face many worrying conditions. Some of the maximum not unusual management traumatic situations embody:

Resistance from others: Leaders may additionally additionally face resistance from others who do not bear in mind their vision or strategies. Leaders need with a view to cope with this resistance and hold to pursue their desires. I can communicate to this once I have encountered opposition and absence of help in a undertaking I have become present technique and the fact that I had an cause, ardour, and purpose I have become capable of live targeted and keep it moving.

•Making difficult picks: Leaders will regularly must make hard choices that might not be famous with every person. These choices may be tough to make, but leaders need for you to stand via their convictions

•Dealing with failure: Leaders will once in a while face failure or lose every other character's take delivery of as actual with, but they ought to investigate from their errors and preserve shifting beforehand sincerely in hopes to rekindle any severed recollect.

These are surely a number of the disturbing conditions that leaders also can face. It is essential for leaders to be prepared for those traumatic conditions and function a plan for a manner to cope with them.

Commit for your principles and values

Now which you have lengthy beyond earlier and characteristic achieved the mini exercising on talents, competencies, and values and indexed a few Essential developments you currently must determine to them and take a look at them in your existence. A capability chief is being born! Principles and values are the topics that you accept as true with in and on the manner to manual your moves as a pacesetter. Leaders want that permits you to articulate their ideas and values in order that others can recognize what they stand for. It is likewise essential that you are regular to your phrases and movements. Being proper is essential for younger leaders. This method being genuine and sincere inside the entirety you do Now that's a real Leader. People will understand you extra in the event that they understand that you are being trustworthy and right.

A private code of ethics and requirements usually protects the inclinations vital for the chief to pursue his or her imaginative and prescient. So having a vision is a crucial aspect of being an effective leader. If you may articulate a clean and galvanizing imaginative and prescient on your future, it is going to be a wonderful deal lots less complicated to advantage others to manual you.

How to extend your control abilties

One manner to begin developing your control competencies is to look at books-I instead advise The Spirit of Leadership and Becoming a Leader by way of way of Dr. Myles Munroe which I actually have mentioned in this financial destroy or articles about control and studying from the critiques of others Attending management workshops or seminars, wherein you can research from professionals inside the subject. You can also exercise your management abilities via leading a collection or a set at college.

Public speaking is a few extraordinary way to expand your control abilities. Practice giving speeches in the the front of a mirror or in the front of small companies of people. If you could talk hopefully within the the front of others, it's far going to be much less hard to guide them. You can be a part of a Toastmasters membership, wherein you could examine and practice public talking.

Another manner to growth your manipulate abilities is to get concerned in volunteering or network company. This is a outstanding manner to assist others and observe control at the identical time. When you are running on duties with others, you'll must find out how to talk successfully, delegate duties, and paintings together as a set. These are all crucial control competencies.

Practice makes development, so the extra you exercise your control skills, the higher you turns into at them. Remember, manipulate is not about perceive or function – it is approximately impact. Anyone may be a pacesetter, regardless of who they're or what they do. It truely takes exercise and resolution.

Chapter 8: Developing Life Skill

Every notable and a success existence flourishes on capacity.

Lack of abilities can kill any profession

Skill connotes apprehend how. It method information and competence. It is the strain at the back of amazing destiny.

Every excellent success is at the mercy of knowledge

As a teenager, there are some records approximately your life and destiny. And the ones facts should be consciously acquired and intelligently carried out in an effort to make high-quality development.

i.In the world we live in nowadays, fine excellence is well known. And it takes capacity to reach at excellence.

ii.Be a learner. You have to research the talent of your future profession. You ought to continuously ask yourself as a youngster this query. What one capability, if I boom and do in an excellent fashion have to have the quality nice effect on my future? Once you are clean about the one expertise as a manner to let you the most, set the purchase of this skills as a cause. Write it down and then artwork to getting better in this location each single day because lack of know-how can kill any super destiny.

iii.Remember this; no person goes to pay on your statistics and your gift. People will constantly pay you on your skills.

And expertise is which include education for your God given information. Many more youthful people are proficient but untrained talented humans. But before your knowledge can income you inside the destiny, it need to have skill and understanding is understanding.

iv.When you have got were given talent, you use a whole lot much less time to benefit a bargain in existence however whilst you don't have functionality you may warfare and advantage a chunk. If you desire to take price of your destiny and your existence, you ought to be expert in dealing with your life.

v.Skill will lessen your sweat and struggles and multiply your fulfillment. Education or having a degree want to now not be incorrect for ability. Skill want to be acquired or your dream in life is probably killed.

vi.The undoing of many younger people these days is un-skillfulness. It is time to move for reality. It is time to buy books and educational CDs. Read all the magazines in your area of interest. Read and examine big. Attend courses and seminars given thru professionals for your area of hobby.

vii. It isn't always just sufficient a super manner to have a incredible dream regarding your destiny. You have to additionally discover ways to reap the dream. Training will growth your ability to excel and be efficient in all which you do.

As a teen, so that it will collect endless success in your future, schooling isn't a desire, it is a must. Don't anticipate it, move for it.

viii. Life capability is a change you take a look at from a practitioner. It should be obtained thru education from the ones who've it. One trouble on the way to make contributions on your success within the destiny is to take time to look at from those who've long past in advance of you. There is no degree of gift or competencies that is alternative for education because of the fact in the good deal you can ever do well; you'll want to analyze it.

ix.Without capability, you can't skip a long manner in life. When you have got had been given capacity, you may be effective.

Chapter 9: Understanding Vision

The oxford advanced dictionary defined imaginative and prescient due to the fact the functionality to endure in mind or plan the future with outstanding imagination and intelligence.

To end up amazing and a achievement, you need to learn to make bigger a passionate life projection. You want to realize the manner to visualize a the following day with normal self assurance.

i.Vision is futuristic and it elements to what you want to come to be within the future. Therefore, allow yourself to dream. Develop a intellectual photo, consider and create the sort of existence you would like to live. As a teen, lifestyles calls so you can apprehend wherein you're going. Life without route is like touring with out vacation spot.

ii.Dream Big! Think Big! And stay like a millionaire you can not be wondering like a slave and live like a king. Every guy's character is a reflected photo of his belief. It is your mind-set that determines your ownership. It is your mentality that set the face in your destiny. My task to you is to start to see along with your inner eyes. Step right into a modern diploma of dwelling. Learn to dream big; in spite of those natural situations outdoor. See a few issue one of a type inner. You can't tour inside and live on a stand no matter the fact that without. Your outside international need to constantly trap up along aspect your inner passion.

iii.Develop a life projection. Life without bearing sincerely turns into stupid and stagnant. What a vision does is to set a future consciousness to help you benefit development. Where there may be no projection, there may be no progression.

Learn to increase a vision for yourself for the form of destiny you desire. When you growth a clean highbrow image of in that you're stepping into existence it gives and infuses power as a manner to enhance sweet motion.

iv.Don't forget about approximately approximately to continually write down your vision. A vision that isn't always documented in writing isn't always any extra than a figment of your imagination.

The shortest pencil is higher than the longest reminiscence. You should have a daily magazine due to the reality until a imaginative and prescient is written. It is not simple! Rather it's miles mysterious, complex and difficult to recognize.

It is surprisingly crucial for your fulfillment in existence which you document every imaginative and prescient and aspiration. They grow to be real and tangible and a few element that you could genuinely reap out to carry out.

v.Break down your vision into smaller, viable, right away and undertakeable dreams. Every vision is a seed. Break it down to a degree that may be taken off. One of the high-quality strategies to actualize your lifestyles imaginative and prescient is so as to get your thoughts off the huge mission within the front of you and reputation on a simple motion that you could take. One of the exquisite strategies to climb the nice mountain is a great manner to take a step at a time. You can accomplish the most important vision on your life with the aid of problem- to take it sincerely one step at a time.

vi.Draw out a path of movement. Planning is your first realistic step towards the realization of your imaginative and prescient. It is not absolutely enough on the way to have a outstanding imaginative and prescient of what you need to turn out to be, you want to also make precise plans for its actualization.

vii. Get set to provide all of it it takes. No lazy individual will ever-revel in proper success. It takes hard paintings to experience brilliant destiny.

Nothing right is available in life except loads of tough art work has preceded the effort.

No temporal achievement is completed thru using taking a short-lessen. There is not any shortcut to lasting achievement.

Hard artwork and diligent pursuit is in the again of every fulfillment in existence.

Take steps in actualizing your vision because all item live at a characteristic of relaxation until a pressure is done. Nothing actions until you bypass.

Even the earth itself is on the flow. It has been in constant movement along its very personal orbit while you don't forget that advent. To be a worthwhile citizen of the earth, you must be in ordinary movement.

Chapter 10: Talent Discovery

i.There is not any ungifted individual in life. Every man and girl, boy and female has a few ability in her or him. All guys are proficient and someone's present is a thing of contact together collectively with his destiny in life. Talents are God's deposits in human vessels. You are endowed for a worthwhile and a tremendous future. You don't have an excuse not to attain life.

ii.You are tremendous made. You have unique capabilities and capabilities that make you exceptional from every other teen. Take stock of your unique competencies and competencies on a normal basis. What is it that you do specially nicely? What are you proper at? Is it music or game? What do you do with out problem and properly that is hard for one-of-a-type people? To make headway in life, you ought to ask yourself "what am I certainly appropriate at, what's going to distinguish me and set me aside as particular and precise in a line up of my buddies?

Look at the numerous assets you do, what is it that you do this gets you the most compliments and reward from one of a kind human beings.

Successful human beings are continuously those who've taken time to find out what they do well and enjoy most. They understand what they are attempting this actually makes a distinction of their lives, and that they then consciousness on that task or vicinity of interest completely.

iii.There is a divine deposit internal of you this is ready to be decided, determined and maximized. Everything God created is blessed with potential. You have already been packaged to be what God desires you to emerge as.

There is a few issue God has placed inner you to make you be triumphant. What a seed desires to turn out to be a tree is already in it. Just display it to the proper environment.

iv.The cause why many younger human beings don't be triumphant is due to the truth they don't accept as true with they personal their dream. Whatever your obligation is in lifestyles, God has built you with the capacity. That's why the Bible says "a man's present maketh room for him" not his training (Pro 18:sixteen). What you've got got internal you is your capability. Discover it, increase it and launch it. It will carry you endless success.

You have inner you a continent of undiscovered potentials; stir it up, launch it and make it provide you with the effects you want. Determine that you are going to provide your fine at each element in time because of the truth the excellent of what you do is a mirrored photo of who you're.

v.As far as God is worried, you are a famous person. No undergo in thoughts in that you are these days or what you are going via, there is a mega-well-known man or woman inner of you.

Begin to look yourself as a first-rate famous character. Refuse to look yourself negatively due to the fact human beings will see you precisely the manner you spot your self. You may be experiencing all way of failure and degradation. However, the truth is that, you are a born massive name. You aren't inferior or nugatory. Many may also have disenchanted you but as a toddler of God, you belong to the very satisfactory diploma of life.

vi.You are designed to hold a completely unique bring about lifestyles. There is some factor in you which God has located there to make you wonderful. You were designed to be someone. You are a e-book to be examine and also you've got to show up. You are a peculiar creature predestined to be a fulfillment; sturdy, fearfully and wonderfully made. You are carefully created. There changed into no mistake in any respect on your creation.

vii.   Awaken the well-known character in you. Find out what you have got inner of you. Discover what you have got been created to perform. Recognize your region of expertise and opt for it!

Chapter 11: Character Formation

Character is all the mental and ethical inclinations that make a person what he is. It is the function that makes a person distinct from others.

i.Character formation is the functions that shape the sample of man or woman behavior. It is the improvement, increase and advancement of an individual life style. The problem of character formation can be very crucial inside the life of a teenager.

ii.Be sincere

Honesty is being truthful in all areas of your life. It manner residing an upright life. Honesty is likewise the tremendous of been clear-cut in life.

Dishonesty is the alternative of honesty

As a teen, you need to discover ways to usually tell the reality. Telling lies will smash your personalities. So keep away from it.

Avoid slander. Because slander will generally make you to free appreciate, dignity and pals.

Don't rob humans of what belongs to them through hints. You gain not anything with the aid of cheating as a substitute you loose all topics at the same time as you live in honesty, you can have a unfastened judgment of right and incorrect with God and man.

iii.Develop moral excellence. This refers in your mode of residing and trendy behavior. Every Christian teen is predicted to excel in his or her ethical existence. Your moral life is depending on your belief, your terms and your deeds.

iv.Always shield your thoughts. You can pleasant manage your body and soul and make stronger your internal man with the useful resource of yielding to God, reading his techniques and counting on his spirit.

The area of your thoughts in person formation can not be overemphasized. The usa of your thoughts affects your character and sample of lifestyles.

You are the control valve of your mind. What you programme into your thoughts is what it feeds you lower back. Positive thoughts produces incredible existence.

v.Be diligent. To be diligent method to be difficult walking.

Diligence reduce inside the direction of every intellectual and bodily realms.

As a Christian youngster, you should have the ability to show everyday try to your research and in a few component you're doing.

Laziness isn't Christianity. So it want to in no manner be part of your individual.

Diligence is your connecting rod to a first rate future.

It could be very important to first artwork together together with your head earlier than you determine along with your hand due to the fact this could prevent from the labour of fools.

vi.Be courageous. Courage is an untiring and undefeatable mind-set. It is born out of willpower. It is an hassle of the heart.

Courage is the functionality to manipulate worry inside the face of hassle or danger.

Never receive defeat.

Reject worry. Don't supply it a preserve for your coronary coronary heart.

You need braveness to actualize your dream. When you personal courage, now not something can be able to intimate you.

vii. Have integrity. Honesty and morality are the two key terms that describe integrity.

A man of integrity is a man this is sincere in dealings and his morally upright.

To stroll in integrity, you want to be contented with what you've got got. Without contentment, loss will maintain coming. Only contentment brings gain.

Live your length consistent with time.

Refuse to stay above your self as an alternative be yourself

viii. Develop non-public concern – This is the outstanding of self control. It is the crucial valve for achievement in lifestyles.

A existence will decay in the absence of difficulty. Don't be in the wrong region, it'll excuse you from wrong act.

ix.Be humble. Always have modest opinion approximately yourself. Humility is the catalyst for a remarkable future.

Chapter 12: Leadership

Everything rises and falls on leadership. The future of any people or tool is largely relying on leadership extraordinary.

i. WHAT IS LEADERSHIP?

Leadership is the potential to encourage and affect a hard and fast of people to acquire a not unusual goal. Leadership isn't always a calling, neither is it a gift, control is earned. People will observe you because they trust they have got something to attract from following you. If you don't have substance you never command goal marketplace.

Leadership can therefore be defined because of the truth the give up fabricated from fulfillment. Commanding followership has no longer some thing to do with age, character, or color. It has nothing to do with position or qualification. It has to do with charge. Many have fallacious control for recognition, however management is an evolution of rate.

There need to be fee that the human beings are after before they let you lead them. Leadership isn't always an endowment, it's miles duty. Leadership isn't in characteristic, it's miles in disposition. That is, improving the fee of your followers.

Leadership is impact.

ii.Increase your price

No count number how talented you're, there may be a place for growth and improvement.

We stay in a global dominated thru civilization, so the volume of statistics you have got got have been given counts. As you enhance your charge, you are enhancing the exceptional of your management. Every main character in any career has paid the price others haven't paid. You want to be willing to go for strategic facts to beautify your control features.

iii.Be devoted for your motive in existence.

Necessity is the mother of invention.

Every certainly committed character may be innovative. Every modern individual can be efficient and every efficient individual is probably a success. Therefore, the fantastic foundation for effective control is willpower to reason.

iv.Be disciplined

Disciplined may be described because the act of submission to the decision for of your set desires.

Only a achievement scholar end up a first rate achiever

You have in all likelihood heard this said before: No Pain; No Gain

This is so actual wherein management is worried. If you need to be a a success chief, you can't have sufficient money to stay simply besides you pick. You have to be someone of vicinity.

Discipline is doing what's demanded and not what's handy.

Discipline requires self-mastery, self-cotnrol, self-obligation and self-order. A disciplined character's existence is ordered and based totally.

v. Have a mentor

There isn't always some thing you may be the next day, that any person has in no way been in advance than. Every greatness is transport by way of way of an present one.

Leadership is a trade; you've got to investigate from the practitioner.

Everyone that desires to be a pacesetter should placed up himself to a mentor to steer his existence.

You need a mentor to store time and strength. There isn't any greatness with out reference. Every son is fathered into greatness.

There isn't any achievement with out reference. Every first-rate chief rises at the shoulder of these in advance of them. Only committed learner will become first-rate leaders. And the cheapest way to analyze is to align your self with individuals who recognize.

vi.Have integrity

Great leaders are commonly very honest with themselves.

Be sincere with your self. Don't misinform yourself.

Leadership isn't always perfection, control is being real.

vii. Be brave. Your capability to make alternatives and to behave boldly on it determines your degree of success in control.

Learn to make desire and stand by using manner of it.

Leadership calls for which you break new ground. To be a fantastic leader, braveness must be your middle name.

Chapter 13: Develop A Positive Value System

Values manner a notion device about what's proper and incorrect and what is vital in life. There are cultural, social and ethical values. You want to learn how to determine your own private values and beliefs.

As a younger person, to assemble a first rate destiny, you ought to enlarge a pleasing value gadget. I consider you have got got heard the area "zero.33 worldwide u . S . A .". We have the primary global and the 0.33 international.

Why are there wonderful "worlds" on one earth? It is due to the fact there may be a cost device, there may be a perception machine and there may be a workout that governs the human beings.

People are not 0.33 international thru accident; they'll be zero.33 global through way of layout and desire. Our worldwide has been normal thru mind, terms and movement. These mind, phrases and moves are although shaping the arena and that is what we referred to as a fee and notion gadget.

i.Therefore, as a way to construct a high-quality future and recreate your global in reality, you have to have and art work for your rate and belief system.

Because you could normally be a fabricated from what you accept as true with.

It has been decided that some values and belief machine are development susceptible and a few are improvement resistance.

ii.Change your spending sample. There are values that resource improvement and there are a few price structures which can be negative.

It's been discovered that for humans to prosper, they should first and major have the capacity to accumulate wealth.

If you have a manner of existence and fee that can not collect wealth, then you can't be wealthy.

Every country that has moved from 1/three worldwide to first international corrected their spending sample and one of the subjects they did changed into to growth the rate and way of life of saving.

When you have were given a charge tool that does not encourage you to hold, poverty will typically be your accomplice.

You want to begin converting your self through way of the usage of converting your price and belief system

iii.Change Your values, form your enchantment and hobby. There are many younger those who can keep in mind every cause scored with the aid of way of their preferred football group in the very last seven years however cannot preserve in mind clean outline from their financial elegance. A lot of teenagers can understand the lyrics in ragge tune however they can't solve the real motives in their failure and setback in university. You can't make rap track your precedence and master your chemistry pocket ebook at the identical time.

iv.Develop a price device that is basically usual by means of the use of the understanding inside the bible and additionally that confirm religion God.

For you to collect a awesome future, the facts of God's phrase should be your every day accomplice. The most important key to success, improvement and civilization is the bible.

The understanding of the Bible isn't always simply so as to memorize verses, the information of the Bible is to create in you a store of records to utility your mind with new records an excellent manner to make you stay to the top of the street that God designed so that it will feature. You need to decide what records this is steady collectively along with your values, in an strive to help you to attain your dream in existence.

v.Work to your concept existence. Everything comes from inside. If you change your notion, you may alternate your coronary coronary heart and in case you change your coronary coronary heart, you'll alternate your future.

It is the brilliant of your thought with a purpose to decide the notable of your existence.

Chapter 14: 5 Habits Of Highly Effective Teens

Habits can be described as obtained mode of conduct. Great achievers have extraordinary behavior. One of the prevailing secrets and strategies and techniques amongst mainly a achievement human beings is reliance upon exact behavior.

As a youngster, developing right behavior will increase your fulfillment, accomplishment, health, shallowness and social have an effect on.

i.Develop behavior of meditation

Meditation may be described because of the truth the act of reasoning, to decide the right steps inside the route of your preferred purpose. It manner to roll over in idea.

Good achievement is continuously tied to meditation. You will become a fulfillment even as you may assume, strategize and meditate.

Every time you adopt the journey of meditation with the whole of your coronary coronary heart, your choice will hold developing toward your vision.

In the college of achievement, outside of strategic thinking, you don't have a destiny. What you have got a observe, what you pay attention and what you observe terrific earnings you with the resource of meditation.

You meditate to understand the proper step and recognize which one may be completed constant with time.

Every discovery and invention in facts is a made of exceptional and analytical wondering.

The guy referred to as Bill Gate have become the richest in the worldwide by manner of motive of strategic thinking, his mind-infant is the Microsoft programme. When he grow to be twelve twelve months antique, his mom modified into looking for him across the residence, Billy, wherein are you, yelled his mum, all of sudden he got here out from one corner of the house and stated, "mama, I am wondering don't you observed'. No wonder, he have emerge as one of the richest men inside the international.

Wealth is a made of man's functionality to assume. If Bill Gates can anticipate his way to stardom on the age of 12, you could do it.

Show me a devoted philosopher and I will display you a superstar inside the making because each celeb is a logician and every truth seeker is a functionality huge call.

ii.Develop the dependancy of self development

Self development is crucial to reaching a excellent destiny due to the fact you could satisfactory boom your truely clearly worth, at the same time as you increase your analyzing.

Your without a doubt worth in lifestyles is truely a characteristic of the manner well knowledgeable you're.

The reason why you need to increase yourself is due to the fact your increase is what determines who you're and who you are determines who you appeal to because of the fact like attraction to like and who you lure determines the success of your non-public dreams.

Achievers are guys that continuously strive for excellence and improvement. They are by no means bored with striving for the fine.

It is not enough as a way to be talented or gifted.

You must additionally advantage knowledge of because of the truth remarkable achievement starts offevolved offevolved with training no longer cash.

Your extraordinary assignment and purpose in existence is to decide what subjects you may do thoroughly and then develop a plan to come to be very, terrific within the ones critical regions.

Your talent is your gift or capacity in its raw form. Unless it is superior or sensitive you can't get the tremendous out of your present. It is private improvement an high-quality manner to refine your talents as gold. Personal improvement will increase your functionality to prosper and be effective in all which you do.

The dependancy of personal development is your guarantee for non-stop achievement and a exceptional future.

iii.   THE   HABIT   OF   PERSONAL RESPONSIBILITY

Your success in lifestyles is largely decided thru you. Not through your mother and father or environments.

Responsibility manner the response of capability to name for located on it. That is, how the capability indoors you responds even as call for is positioned on it.

Responsibility is a awesome of being reliable, reliable and accountable, answerable and consider worth. When you supply a while, electricity and attention in your studies, career and your God given venture, you're on your way to experience wonderful step forward.

There are a few capabilities God has deposited inner you and till they start to find expression through you doing what you can do with what you've got were given, in which you are, you could in no way be fulfilled.

Until you assignment the ones competencies interior you, they'll not discover expression. Those abilities had been placed there through God, however you need to allow them to go along with the go with the flow out.

You will in no way apprehend the extent to which you may carry out till you respond to the demands and people desires are what we name challenges.

iv. DEVELOP THE HABIT OF PLANNING

As a teen, to assemble a notable destiny, you need to build the dependancy of planning. Because to fail to devise, is to plan to fail.

Your dream, irrespective of how noble and amazing it is, will no longer see the mild of the day without proper planning.

Planning is your first practical step in the route of the belief of your dream. You attain subjects speedy thru manner of wondering and making plans in advance and on foot with available statistics.

v. HABIT OF TAKING POSITIVE ACTION

Every item assumes a kingdom of relaxation until an out of doors applicable pressure is performed to it. Nothing movements till you circulate. Achievers don't look ahead to matters to move lower back to them, they usually move after them.

Successful humans don't procrastinate. Action not on time is future behind schedule and future not on time is the satan's pride.

When you have were given were given decided what you need to do, act on it straight away. Strike whilst the iron is warm! Never take away till tomorrow, what you have to do in recent times. Tomorrow may be too late!

Chapter 15: Entrepreneurship

Oxford superior dictionary defined entrepreneur as someone who makes cash via starting or taking walks agency, particularly at the same time as this involved taking financial dangers.

There are unique breeds of entrepreneurs steady with Robert G. Allen the writer of "Nothing Down". He named them as follows.

INTRAPRENEUR: If you're pinnacle at influencing the selection of others; if you like giving hints to others, in case you revel in selling, you are an intrapreneur.

INFOPRENEUR: if you experience organizing and simplifying information; in case you enjoy schooling; in case you enjoy public talking. In case you revel in writing; if you want to take a look at; if you are an idea person, you are an infopreneur.

AUTOPRENEUR: If you revel in seeing your coins develop at the same time as you sleep; in case you need to make gives; in case you experience locating bargains; if you need to personal subjects; in case you are appropriate at comparing excellent tasks and houses to come to a decision, you qualify to be an autopreneur.

The relevance of entrepreneurship is not any doubt a topic that ought to benefit know-how of to each youngster over and over again. Most a hit humans in America these days commenced out their corporation at a very more youthful age. Young people should be made to see the significance of free agency. This, I obtain as real with is one of the crucial keys to constructing a wealthy economic machine.

i.As a teen, your adventure toward entrepreneurship want to begin with a clean choice: A desire to grow to be financially impartial. There are such masses of things that could make you need to grow to be financially unbiased. It might be due to the reality you preference to make more money; it is able to be because of the fact you preference to particular your self or due to the fact you want to introduce new mind, harm a file or make a distinction within the society. It can also be because of the truth you want to assist your family or make contributions to the building of community trends together with colleges, hospitals and so on.

ii.Recognize the power of concept.

Idea is the place to start of all agency success. Every invention, enterprise, enterprise, employer, company, product that we've got these days, happened due to one man's or female's idea. The handiest fantastic manner to emerge as a a fulfillment entrepreneur is to provide you with a notable idea.

iii.Have a mentor

A mentor is someone who advises and trains a person of lesser experience, called a protégé. When you are related to a mentor, it gives you better degree of facts. This is the crucial key to the unusual fulfillment of many a success human beings.

The fastest manner to emerge as a splendid entrepreneur is to test from those who've lengthy lengthy past in advance.

iv.Has a passion

Passion is to crave or extended for some component with intensity. To grow to be a a hit entrepreneur, you want to have a burning desire to accumulate wealth. A mild choice or informal interest isn't always sufficient.

Passion is an vital requirement for employer achievement. It changed into the passion of being a international diagnosed scientist that drove Albert Einstein and Isaac Newton and all those renowned scientist to persist and persevere in their studies and theories until a jump in advance grow to be found.

v.Have a focus

To make the maximum of your lifestyles and business employer, you need to understand the principle of cognizance. To enjoy incredible fulfillment as an entrepreneur, you ought to in reality perceive and hobby on your challenge. You want to apprehend the cause why you are in business enterprise and recognition on it throughout.

Bill Gate modified into a university student who on the equal time changed into already making superb in roads into the computer software program program agency. However, he didn't just want to make great inroads, he desired to create a revolution within the industry. So he dropped out of university to stand the software program program improvement business business organisation complete time. He already knew all what changed into wished for him to improve in enterprise. He knew that staying on at the college may not growth his possibilities of achievement in commercial enterprise commercial enterprise business enterprise. So he decided to drop out. He went onto construct the largest laptop software program software business business enterprise in the global and moreover turn out to be the vicinity's richest man inside the approach. He didn't need a university degree to do all that. He is now stated to have determined to transport decrease returned and whole the abandoned university degree. That is an instance of the electricity of recognition.

Chapter 16: Money Management

The phrase of God says, "There is treasure to be favored and oil within the living of the sensible; however a silly guy spendeth it up. (Proverbs 21:20)

If you need to gather economic freedom in existence, you want to learn how to manual your affairs with discretion. You should learn how to manipulate your cash accurately. Robert Kiyosaki, renowned writer of Rich Dad Poor Dad said, "Money without monetary intelligence is money speedy prolonged past".

i.If genuine riches are your purpose, you need to be financially literate on the way to control your finance correctly. Learn to make investments your coins effectively.

ii.Always set apart a number of your income for both your religious investment and bodily funding through the use of giving 10 man or woman of your income to God within the tithe and to position 10 percentage into your destiny in fixed deposit or inventory market.

Don't wait until you have got a lump of amount of money earlier than you begin the method of making an investment. Start in which you're, with what you've got.

It is a easy principle of economic fortune. There has in no way been someone who has finished superb financial achievement with out sensible funding.

iii.Be frugal

Frugality is the cautious and smart use of cash, assets and possibilities. Frugality is the gateway to wealth creation. A frugal character is a person who cautiously and as it should be makes use of the cash and aid at his or her disposal.

You want to lessen your spending pattern that allows you to assemble wealth for the future. Don't be deceived via the usage of some of the belongings you look beforehand on your TV, internet and cable. Many human beings residing in America in recent times are living in debt. They recall in spending the next day's cash these days.

iv.Be sincere

Remember, the bible says to him who is sincere shall more be delivered and to him that is unfaithful inside the little even the little he has may be taken from him and given to him that has more.

So, be enterprising with the little at your disposal and you could enjoy growth and multiplication.

Part of proper control is retaining a budget of all your fees.

You want this budgetary approach to grow to be an outstanding and a fulfillment supervisor of fortune.

v.Be devoted

It takes faithfulness to enjoy economic freedom.

The bible says in proverb 28:20, "a devoted guy shall abound with blessing, but he that maketh haste to be wealthy shall not be innocent.

Faithfulness is coping with the small as correctly because of the truth the big. It is setting your pleasant into what you're doing. In one-of-a-type words, shopping for and promoting with what you have got got had been given.

Faithfulness is putting in your great in what you're doing now. It is buying and selling what you have got got for boom.

In the college of economic achievement, faithfulness is a check you need to bypass in advance than your greatness arrives. Make the most of the available belongings at your disposal in keeping with-time. It isn't always a feature of tactics plenty is available however a function of ways nicely you can manage it.

vi.Maintain your degree

Life is in stages and men are in sizes.

Those who live above their way and level continuously end up stealing.

Wisdom call for that you do now not live your the following day today. The first-rate friend anybody ought to have is CONTENTMENT.

Learn to order your priorities right and stay interior your way consistent with time. When you live above your technique you will stay in lack and need and this can lead you into begging and borrowing.

Chapter 17: Time And Life Management

There is not any real excellence on this international that can be separated from proper dwelling. And right living starts from facts the essence of lifestyles. Time is the essence of lifestyles.

TIME IS LIFE

Proper control of it sluggish in recent times will continuously assure a excellent future.

i.What is time?

Time is the series of sports relative to the clock.

ii.Establish your price

What will you be willing to take a risk for? What are the thinks that drives you.

If you don't installation your fee, people will provide you with their very own price.

Your fee will constantly have an impact to your alternatives in life.

What are the property you rate loads about life.

Your every day activities want to replicate your private cost.

You must ought to make a listing or motion listing ordinary.

iii.Always set desires to your existence

Goal putting will will let you seize time. Without desires, existence is complete of frustration.

All the first-rate achievers inside the global generally set their priorities through reason placing. As a teenager, to have a super destiny, you need to have very smooth, concise goals in lifestyles. A experience of private task will deliver the feeling of urgency to perform and acquire your desires on time.

iv.Avoid searching the tv whenever or for prolonged hours.

The impact of the television revolution cannot be underneath anticipated on these days's young adults. Television has in recent times become the undoing of many greater younger people.

Quality time that is meant to be used in reading, wondering and planning for the destiny is spent looking track channels and immoral films.

Ben Carson, a worldwide famend Pediatric Neuro Surgeon and the writer of the nice promoting e-book "THINK BIG" said in his testimony.

'I became likely the worst pupil you've ever seen. I idea I emerge as surely stupid. All my classmate and instructors agreed, and my nickname emerge as "Dummy", however like many students, I type of expected myself as a health practitioner anyway and I hung on to that dream, notwithstanding the fact that I wasn't doing nicely.

My mother changed into horrified at the same time as she discovered my file card at mid-time period within the fifth grade. I became failing almost every difficulty. She knew what a hard lifestyles she had, searching for to beautify two extra younger sons inside the inner town without a sources. She located my brother and I heading down the equal direction. She certainly didn't apprehend what to do.

She prayed for facts and got here up with the concept of turning off the tv set and letting us watch handiest or three pre-selected TV applications at a few level in the week. And with all of that spare time we needed to examine books a piece from the Detroit public library and placed up to her written e-book evaluations…….

We had to live in the house and have a look at the ones books at the same time as our buddies were outside and that they were playing. I hated it for the first numerous weeks, however then all of a surprising, I started out out to enjoy it, because…..We had no money, however among the cover of these books, I may additionally additionally want to transport anywhere, I can be sincerely absolutely everyone, I need to do a little thing.

I began to use my creativeness greater, because it doesn't definitely require quite some imagination to observe tv, however it does to examine…..Within a rely of a 12 months and a 1/2 I went from the lowest of the elegance to the top of the magnificence, lots to the consternation of all of the ones college students who used to tease me and call me names…..Once I identified that I had the ability to pretty a excellent deal to map out my private future based mostly on the selection I made, and the diploma of strength I located into it, life becomes first-rate from that thing.

Chapter 18: Goals Setting And How To Do It Well

As a teen or more youthful person, it's far key that you understand what you want. You may additionally moreover understand what you want but no longer a manner to benefit it.

That's where purpose placing is to be had in. Goals help you recommend for the destiny and play an crucial function in talents improvement in all aspects of lifestyles. They are our goals and goal we plan to actualise.

When you recognize the importance of desires and the way to set them, it'll located you on the right route to achievement.

According to "Pablo Picasso" – "Our dreams can great be reached through a car of a plan, in which we want to vigorously act. There isn't another direction to success"

What is Goal Setting?

Goals are the object or intention of an motion. For example, they will be particular goals we plan to reap and determine in competition to a benchmark or fashionable. The machine of achieving those desires is known as aim setting. The importance of motive setting cannot be over-emphasized. Our lives depend on the process of selecting the wants to pursue; if not accomplished successfully, can affect your achievement in existence. We ought to decide what is important to us and set goals to gain them.

Researchers have positioned that some humans perform higher than others even as performing the identical assignment. The motive for this has been related to the motivations of the 2 organizations of human beings. The diploma of motivation exhibited depends on the overall performance of dreams. What this indicates is that setting dreams can significantly have an impact on performance.

Why is Goal Setting crucial?

As noted earlier, the dreams we set increase motivation and strength of will. In addition, goals have an impact at the intensity of our actions and feelings. The diploma of trouble in attaining the intention determines the quantity of try we installed to accumulate it and therefore, the greater the fulfillment we enjoy.

When we enjoy success and powerful emotions because of attaining dreams, our self notion and perception in our private capability increase. It is a high-quality idea to take part in motive putting as this may encourage you to find out new strategies or novel methods to benefit them.

The capability to devise substantially have an effect on perceived manage over the consequences.

Key Principles of Goal Setting

Having specific wants to benefit produces higher performance in assessment to even as there aren't any particular desires. In other words, when we set honestly described desires, we're much more likely to attain them.

There are 5 requirements for a hit purpose putting (Locke & Latham, 1990). These are Commitment, Clarity, Challenge, Complexity and Feedback. Now allow us to communicate those 5 requirements and have a look at how they assist goal placing.

Commitment

Commitment is related to the extent of attachment an man or woman has to the cause and the willpower behind it – irrespective of the constraints. Lockie & Latham (1990) located that people carry out better on their goals whilst they may be dedicated or maybe higher while the goals are tough.

When you're commuted to a purpose and also you discover your standard overall performance isn't always up to scratch, you're probably to increase try or exchange procedures to reap them. On the opportunity hand, at the same time as you're a brilliant deal much less committed to goals – in particular tough dreams – you're probable to give up o them. Therefore, whilst there can be dedication, and the possibilities of attaining desires are better.

Some factors can affect our self-discipline diploma, those elements consist of the perceived desire for the cause and the perceived functionality to obtain it (Miner, 2005).

Clarity

When dreams are clear and particular, it's far much less complex to comply with in comparison to on the same time as dreams are indistinct. Vague desires do not encourage determination. Therefore, it's far important to set smooth, unique and unambiguous dreams which is probably measurable. When we are clean on the aim we plan to acquire, the preferred mission is thought. The ensuing fulfillment that includes this is moreover a source of motivation.

Challenging

Goals are expected to be tough but viable in any other case, the self-discipline to reap them can be lost. When goals are hard, overall performance can be improved as pleasure is accelerated along motivation to discover the right strategies to attain them (Locke & Latham, 1990).

Task Complexity

The challenge required for executing dreams does now not need to be complicated. When dreams are past our functionality degree, they will be overwhelming and negatively have an impact on our morale.

This is why the time scale to reap goals want to be practical in any other case, we often lose motivation and fail to collect desires.

Feedback

Goal placing may be more powerful while there may be feedback (Erez, 1977). Feedback can be useful in assessing development to accomplishing desires. However, feedback needs to be as smooth as viable in distinctive to permit motion to be taken.

When fundamental overall performance isn't always at the extent expected to gain a cause, remarks lets in movement to be taken and new possible desires to be set. In the absence of feedback, it'll probably be tough to evaluate the effectiveness of the techniques in a properly timed manner that may sluggish improvement (Zimmerman, 2008).

Knowing that we have become closer to our goals offers us that brought push to research a modern-day capacity and set greater difficult goals.

8 Interesting Facts on gaol Setting

1.Setting desires and reflecting on them helps the instructional achievement

2.Goals inspire you to attain achievement

3.Goals placing maintains you within the exquisite kingdom of thoughts to carry out effectively.

4.When you hold an wonderful method to reason placing, it drives you to acquire success.

5.Goals which might be specific yet difficult cause progressed overall performance.

6.People with excessive capacity are much more likely to set hard desires and note them to completion.

7.Social have an effect on performs a massive function in purpose alternatives.

eight.Goal putting is a powerful tool to encourage really as monetary incentives.

Skills Required for Goal Setting

There are vital competencies preferred that could extensively decorate goal putting and its success. These abilties may be located out and with out trouble superior through operating toward them. If you locate gaol placing difficult, it is able to be that you are lacking this kind of competencies.

•Planning

Planning is important in terms of intention putting. Through planning, we're able to prioritize and organise task which is wanted in the course of purpose placing. When we plan, we are much more likely to stay focussed at the undertaking and no longer get distracted.

•Self-Motivation

Self-motivation is needed if desires are to be completed. There want to be that preference otherwise the motive is destined to fail from the start. In the method of executing our dreams, we can also face worrying situations or opposition, having self-motivation guarantees we find out solutions to the ones demanding situations as we navigate our way.

•Time manipulate

Time manipulate expertise is constantly a excellent capability to have. Allowing for appropriate enough time to attain goals is important, in any other case, the assignment may match unfinished.

•Flexibility

In life subjects don't usually drift the way we want. When this happens, we want to take a step again and re-examine our dreams and if vital, revise and set new goals.

•Self-regulation

We all need the capacity to self-modify or control our feelings.

•Commitment and Focus

As highlighted earlier willpower is prime and dedication is what will maintain you going whilst sooner or later of difficult instances. If we are related to a purpose we would be geared up to move all out to see it out.

SMART Goals

Smart stands for Specific, measurable, conceivable, applicable and time particular. The clever framework ensures that dreams are the wonderful they may be. Let us in short have a study each of those letters.

•Specific

Goals want to be as precise as they may be. Open-ended dreams can bring about frustration. The brilliant way to examine it's far to apprehend what, why, at the same time as and the manner of the intention. What is the cause, whilst is the aim to be carried out and the way is it to be completed?

•Measurable

Having a metric by the use of which to degree your improvement can be very vital as this lets in music progress. Suppose the intention is to shed kilos then the metric may be your weight in Kilogramme.

•Achievable / Attainable

Goals ought to be capability otherwise it's miles going to be a failed mission. Sometimes we would have lofty mind however this needs to be knowledgeable via our capability and capabilities to accumulate them. For example, if you plan to be an professional in a far off places language in 2 weeks. This is incredible for max humans.

•Relevant/ sensible

The desires we set ought to be relevant. If it isn't always applicable, we need to emerge as putting desires that fulfil no longer some thing on the end of the day. There must be a why? For every task.

•Time-Specific

Goals need to be time-bound in any other case the mission can bypass on for all time. Allocating time to the intention permits us to evaluate on the identical time as the time is reached and hold us attention on carrying out the intention.

Steps to Setting Goals

1.Think about the effects you need to look

2.Create SMART desires

3.Write your dreams down

four.Create an movement plan

5.Create a timeline

6.Take motion

7.Re-compare and asses your development

Chapter 19: Personal Health

Eating a Balanced Diet

Eating a balanced food plan is an important a part of your non-public health and will make revel in your great. A balanced eating regimen offers your frame all the vitamins it goals. Nutrients come from energy.

A balanced diet plan involves ingesting a large sort of additives within the proper percentage and ingesting the correct quantity of food to hold a wholesome lifestyle.

Calories in meals talk with the power stored in food. It is the electricity in food our body makes use of at the same time as we perform most sports activities like strolling, walking or swimming. The common individual desires approximately 2000 calories to maintain them going every day. However, it is predicated upon on age, intercourse and interest degree.

See the table beneath for a manual on the extensive shape of energy required for one-of-a-type agencies. Source – "healthcare.Com".

Person

Calorie necessities

Sedentary children: 2–eight years

1,000–1,four hundred

Active children: 2–eight years

1,000–2,000

Females: 9–13 years

1,four hundred–2,two hundred

Males: nine–13 years

1,six hundred–2,600

Active women: 14–30 years

2,4 hundred

Sedentary ladies: 14–30 years

1,800–2,000

Active person men: 14–30 years

2,800–3,two hundred

Sedentary men: 14–30 years

2,000–2,600

Active human beings: 30 years and over

2,000–three,000

Sedentary humans: 30 years and over

1,six hundred–2,4 hundred

The source of energy is important. Some food provide little or no nutrients however lots of power. These elements are known as "empty energy"

Examples of meals with empty power are;

•Sodas

•Pizza

•Ice cream

•Chips and fries

•Processed meat

•Cakes, cookies and doughnuts

•Fruit liquids with brought sugar

Food Groups and Your Diet

To have a wholesome eating regimen, you want to have the subsequent companies of meals;

•Eat five portions shape of fruit and greens every day

•Eat food with higher fibre, ie, potatoes, rice, bread or pasta

•Take a few dairy or its options which encompass soya milk

•Add protein on your food including beans, fish, eggs

•Take unsaturated oils and spreads in small amount

•Drink masses of beverages at least up to eight glasses an afternoon

Try to reduce your intake of meals with immoderate portions of fat, salt and sugar. Too a first-rate deal of this meals isn't always unique in your health.

Fruit and vegetables

It is suggested that fruit and veggies have to make up approximately a 3rd of the meals you consume each day as they're an fantastic deliver of nutrients and minerals.

As said earlier, five portions of fruit and veggies are recommended every day and that they'll be sparkling, frozen canned, dried or juiced.

Doctors and researchers endorsed this restriction primarily based totally on proof that folks that observe this normal have a tendency to have a lower danger of heart sickness, stroke and positive cancer.

Examples of part of fruit and veggies are;

•1 apple, banana, pear or comparable.

•A slice of melon or pineapple

•A tablespoon of dry fruit to cereals

•80g of canned, clean, or frozen fruit.

•30 g of dried fruit

•150ml glass of juice or smoothie

Why a balanced Diet is vital?

A balanced food plan gives the nutrients our frame desires to art work efficiently. In the absence of a balanced diet, our frame can be liable to disease, contamination, fatigue and espresso ordinary normal overall performance.

It is extensively identified that kids who do now not eat healthful also can face boom and development problems, terrible performance at university and a excessive risk of infection. In addition, terrible consuming behavior can be advanced which kids take into adulthood.

Food to Avoid

•Processed food

•Food with brought Sugar

•Red and Processed meat

•Alcohol

Exercises

According to specialists Children elderly 6 – 17 require as a minimum one hour of physical workout each day to assist optimise health. There are techniques to get your frame active which incorporates taking a walk, on foot, the use of a bike or going to the park and attractive in severa sports together with skipping ropes and mountaineering. Starting a routine early is essential as it's miles more much less complicated to take into maturity.

First Aid Basics

Learning first useful aid techniques will help you deal with an emergency. You may also additionally hold someone breathing and decrease their ache while an ambulance is on its way. It is probably the difference amongst lifestyles and lack of lifestyles for plenty.

When it involves first resource, the acronym DRSABCD is to be observed;

•D stands for Danger – Check there may be no threat to you

•R stands for Response – Check that the individual is aware

•S stands for Send for assist

•A stand for Airways – Is the man or woman's airways smooth

•B stands for respiratory – Check that the character is breathing through looking for chest movement up and down

•C stands for CPR – Cardiopulmonary Resuscitation – If the man or woman isn't always breathing, ensure they are flat on their again. Then area the heel of one hand at the centre in their chest and your hands on top. Press down firmly up and down 30 times. Provide breaths. While giving the breath through the mouth, ensure that their head is tilted backwards and pinch their nose. Repeat the technique till you notice signs and symptoms of respiratory.

•B stand for Defibrillator – This is used for subconscious adults who aren't breathing. These are available in plenty of public places. Follow the instructions

Chapter 20: Home Maintenance

Our domestic is normally our biggest asset and some thing may be completed to hold it is a welcome development. Lack of protection may want to make matters precious lose rate because of deterioration. Therefore, maintaining the house may be very essential. The actual trouble is domestic renovation can experience like a frightening assignment however with steering and the proper machine, it makes existence plenty tons less complicated.

What we need to endure in thoughts is that a home operates with seasons, coming to lifestyles in spring and then regularly stepping into wintry weather. In extraordinary phrases, what we look out for in spring is pretty tremendous in wintry weather. The equal is going for summer season and then fall.

Spring

Spring is the time we need to depart our home windows and begin cleansing our closets. Giving your property internal and out an outstanding easy down is all that is in our thoughts.

•Grounds

It is beneficial to begin out of doors raking up leaves that fell off due to the dry climate from wintry weather. If possible, get a few mulch and lay them down on available soil. Muclch is fabricated from tree backs or woods. Mulch allows guard vegetation from drought and keep weeds at bay. You can mow your lawn if you need to and if wished renew your agreement for lawn mowing offerings.

•Trees

Trees want to be checked to peer if they will be loss of existence. If you are not conversant with identifying contamination in a dying tree, get a certified arborist. A loss of life tree can also moreover need to pose a protection hazzard to you if not caught early.

•Lawns and hedges

This is the time to reseed your garden and top off all of the bald patches in advance than the summer season warmness. Perennials moreover need to be planted and given masses of water. Sometimes you could need fertiliser for your vegetation. If so, get a few and add it to the soil to help provide vitamins

•Snowblower and lawnmower

As iciness is now over, it's time to save your snow blower. Drain the gasoline and or add a stabilizer and clean and check the additives. Then pull out your lawnmower and deliver it a take a look at up earlier than the grass get too prolonged. Lawnmower do pretty some work however do not get all the love. If viable despatched it out for a take a look at. Blades may additionally

additionally need to be sharpened, plugs changed and pressure belts changed.

•Outside of the Home

Inspect the thru strolling around the residence. You also can examine cracks within the concrete. Also test the strain manner is in suitable scenario. Check the roof for signs and symptoms and symptoms and signs and symptoms and symptoms of tear or holes.

Inspect the gutters to look if there are any blockages preventing the float of rain water from your roof siding and foundations. When gutters are clogged, it can motive roof to leak or water to infiltrate the house. The gutter need to be wiped easy at the least two times a 12 months or extra frequently counting on the residence plan and bushes round.

•Paint

Look for signs and symptoms of peeling and chipping of paint. Paints are suitable at preserving your outdoor searching extremely good and can shield your facility from water harm or rot. It is generally encouraged to get painting finished as quick as feasible by using the use of forestall of summer season.

•Patio / Deck

Sweep all patios clean to remove any undesirable layer deposits. Inspect the deck looking for symptoms of cracked timber and so on.

•Inside Your Home

For houses with HVAC systems with major warmth and air, that may be a awesome time to call your technicians to get it checked for any symptoms and signs and symptoms of damage, and easy and provider the furnace and compressors.

Boilers want to be checked and serviced to smooth out any amassed sediment.

Pipes want to be checked specifically underneath the sink to ensure there are not any symptoms of a leak. Look up the ceilings and walls for telltale water stains which is an indication of a leak in the wall.

Finally, test your chimneys. You need to take a look at them even in case you don't use the fireside often. According to the chimney safety institute of America, chimneys need to be inspected yearly and wiped clean periodically.

Summer

We all look in advance to summer season as it is the season to experience your private home. However, some chores however need to be completed to hold the house jogging. If we're capable of hold on top of these chores, there will nevertheless be time for barbecues and sunbathing.

•Grounds

Start with the garden. Bring out the garden mower and set to the exceptional placing so as not to reduce grass too quick and divulge the garden to weeds. Remove every weed wherein relevant. It is also time to start to water the plant life and plants.

•Pools

Try to keep your pool clean via the use of skimming the surface often to keep leaves and particles away. Check the edges and scrub if need be and in addition to the filters and chemical degree. You additionally want to maintain a watch constant on the water diploma.

•Inside Your Home

Clean air-conditioning gadgets inner and out. Prepare for severe warmth. Heat waves can stress electricity traces so make sure to prepare for all scenarios and stock the residence with batteries and flashlights. Get can meals, remedy and number one resource kits.

In case of emergency, have a plan. Take phrase of emergency cell phone lines and feature an evacuation plan organized.

Get rid of insects and pests. Termites call for professional help to curtail so don't hesitate to call for assist. Seal all holes that may end up get right of entry to elements for mice. Check the artic or loft regularly.

Check if there are domestic upgrades to be completed as most contractors want to carry out outside projects inside the direction of the summer time.

Fall

This is the time to start to put together for wintry weather. For the ones in a warmer climate, there may be usually very little to do at this stage.

•Grounds

According to professionals, fall is the awesome time to plant bushes and shrubs and reseed your lawn. Try to water your plants earlier than they cross dormant, in order that by using spring you could get the primary bloom. The praise for planting the wood is probably surely well worth it whilst they arrive alive in spring.

As you may understand, this is additionally even as leaves start to fall off from bushes and you want to get the rake out. However, don't overburden yourself looking for to put off all leaves as a moderate rake will do certainly extraordinary. It may additionally interest you to recognize that leaving some leaves within the once more of is virtually help defend the garden in the course of wintry weather. The leaves furthermore offer protection for bugs and herbal international.

•Outside the Home

Due to the leaves falling, gutters end up clogged and want to be cleared. All protection that want to be finished want to be finished as possible earlier than winters devices in. Roof need to be inspected for any lose or damaged tiles.

All sprinklers have to be near down a to defend is from harsh weather. Shut off the water deliver to the irrigation. System. Insulate any valve and drain any last water from the machine.

If you operate firewood to your chimney. This is the time to inventory up. They should be stacked on pallets in order that they do now not have contact with the wet floor. Cover the wooden up to save you fungus from developing on them. Bear in mind that wooden draws bugs so do now not hold them inside the house for additonal than in keeping with week.

Clean, close to and cowl swimming pools to put together for wintry weather.

•Inside Your Home

Air-conditioning devices and furnaces must be serviced at some stage in this era. Ensure boilers and radiators are working properly. Check and update filters if crucial. Test the thermostat and take a look at the heating vents are open and no longer the usage of a blocks.

Also, check that smoke and carbon monoxide detectors are in correct walking circumstance.

Winter

As it is also very bloodless in wintry climate, little or no domestic development may be performed in some unspecified time in the future of this era. This is why we want to be prepared for harsh weather conditions.

•Ground

This is the time to supply out snow blowers. Ensure that it is in wonderful operating state of affairs in advance than it snows.

Keep the shovels near in the occasion it will become vital. Stock up assets, which includes any ice-melting merchandise.

•Inside Your Home

Check your boilers and mainly, the pressure at the gauge as can require to be crowned up otherwise boiler may not begin.

Check for frozen pipes. When pipes freeze they'll increase and settlement most important to cracking.

Have a generator available and it could be a lifeline inside the occasion of a blackout. Keep fuel and oil in garage outdoor. Check tank storage often for placed on and tear.

www.ingramcontent.com/pod-product-compliance
Lightning Source LLC
Chambersburg PA
CBHW071336120626
46546CB00002B/583